BACCARAT
for the
CLUELESS

BACCARAT
for the
CLUELESS

John May

A LYLE STUART BOOK
Published by Carol Publishing Group

A Lyle Stuart Book
Published by Carol Publishing Group
Lyle Stuart is a registered trademark of Carol Communications, Inc.

Editorial, sales and distribution, and rights and permissions inquiries should be addressed to Carol Publishing Group, 120 Enterprise Avenue, Secaucus, N.J. 07094.

In Canada: Canadian Manda Group, One Atlantic Avenue, Suite 105, Toronto, Ontario M6K 3E7

Carol Publishing Group books may be purchased in bulk at special discounts for sales promotion, fundraising, or educational purposes. Special editions can be created to specifications. For details, contact Special Sales Department, Carol Publishing Group, 120 Enterprise Avenue, Secaucus, N.J. 07094.

Manufactured in the United States of America

10 9 8 7 6 5 4 3 2 1

Library of Congress Cataloging-in-Publication Data

May, John.
    Baccarat for the clueless / John May.
        p. cm.
    "A Lyle Stuart book."
    ISBN 0–8184–0604-6 (pbk.)
    1. Baccarat I. Title.
GV1295.B3M39 1998
795.4'2—dc21   98–19278
                                CIP

Dedicated to the memory of
Jadwiga Helena Szanser
(1913–96)

CONTENTS

I was continually overwhelmed by one powerful thought: you have already concluded that it is possible to become a millionaire with absolute certainty, if only one has sufficient strength of character... And I still retain the conviction that in games of chance if one is absolutely calm, so that one's powers of discrimination and calculation are unimpaired, it is impossible not to overcome the crudity of blind chance and win.

Dostoyevsky, *The Gambler*

BACCARAT
for the
CLUELESS

1

Introduction

What is baccarat? Its essence is best transmitted in the evocative imagery the word conjures—wealth, glamour, and taste. It is the game of the high roller par excellence, the type of gambler who bets in the thousands or tens of thousands. It is the cordoned off area where the ordinary players gather and gasp at the huge risks that can leave a player better or worse off by over a million dollars in a single session. It is the game of tuxedoed dealers and plush opulence. It is James Bond in *Casino Royale* or Robert Redford in *Indecent Proposal*. It is the chandeliers, the immaculate croupiers, the focus of all the pampered luxury the casino industry can muster. It is exclusiveness personified— the game which gamblers play in order to show their status and power, to show that extreme turns of fate, gains or losses, do not affect them as they would ordinary men. It has been the downfall of many ruined aristocrats. It is, perhaps, the most seductive and gentle road to penury.

This book is quite unlike anything else you have read or are ever likely to read on the subject. To my knowledge, it is the most comprehensive treatment of the game available. If you have a question about baccarat, the answer is likely to be here, or the question has yet to be answered. This book should be useful for the complete novice, but it contains much that is new for the seasoned gambler. I also answer the oldest questions man has asked since the first bone dice were manufactured some time back in prehistory: Can you beat the odds?

Aside from a few dusty technical papers hidden away in university libraries, no complete study of the modern form of baccarat has been written. The mysteries of the baccarat deck are myriad, deep, and impenetrable. Few gamblers understand the subtleties of the game. This book may hopefully shed some light on the highest stage of gambling. Baccarat is a game that takes minutes to learn how to play, but its subtleties could very well take a lifetime to understand.

Can I Play Baccarat?

Yes, this is the twentieth century. You don't have to be a high roller. You don't even have to understand the rules properly. Just don't allow anyone to intimidate you. As long as you put down the table minimum, you are welcome to play baccarat in any casino where the game is offered.

You might say, "I don't know anything about cards!" Well, you don't need to. In fact, that's probably an advantage. Skill is of no importance to most baccarat players. There are skillful strategies that can help you beat the house, and I will explain some of them. Most players, however, treat the game as what it is: a coin toss with a lot of impressive ritual, which may be glamorous, attractive, amusing, but is essentially unnecessary.

Why should you play baccarat when the odds are stacked in the house's favor? Well, first, because playing baccarat is in itself an experience worth paying a little for. Second, while the house does have the edge, its advantage is very small in comparison to other games. Third, if you read this book, *you* can have the edge over the casino. Finally, there are few areas of life where the odds are not stacked against you, as anyone who's ever had a bad experience with a bank manager, real estate agent, or insurance company should know—and *they* don't pay for your drinks. In baccarat, you must have a positive mental attitude to succeed. If you think you will lose, you have already lost before you set foot in the casino. Don't impose needless limitations on yourself. Go for the chandeliers!

How to Play Baccarat

The following is a brief description of the typical baccarat procedure. While this should explain the basic structure of the game, players should be aware that the fine details surrounding the game proper can vary not only from one country to another, but from casino to casino.

As in all casino games, you must first transfer your cash into gaming chips, sometimes called "checks." There are obvious practical disadvantages in playing with cash. In America, almost all casinos use red to symbolize $5 chips, green to represent $25 chips, and black for $100 chips.

Often the baccarat section of a casino may be cordoned off, or be in a room of its own. This tends to intimidate many would-be players; it also caters to the whims of the high roller who does not want to be surrounded by ordinary gamblers. In order to sit at the table, it is best to know the table minimum beforehand. If this is not clearly signposted, you may have to ask casino personnel, which leaves you open to the reply, "If you have to ask—you can't afford it!" A typical minimum is rarely less than $20, however, in Nevada you may find $5 minimums. The baccarat table usually seats twelve players, plus three dealers, two of whom deal with payoffs and chip collection.

Often there will be a beautiful female "shill" playing. A shill is a casino employee who poses as an ordinary player in order to make other players feel less self-conscious about approaching the table. The shills play with house money (they don't get to keep it if they win) and do not affect the game in any way. If you feel there are shills at the table and are uncomfortable with this, simply ask if this is the case, and the casino must, by law, tell you.

The third dealer, known as the caller, deals out instructions to the players, and passes the "shoe" after each hand. The shoe is a wooden box used to hold decks of cards in all casino games.

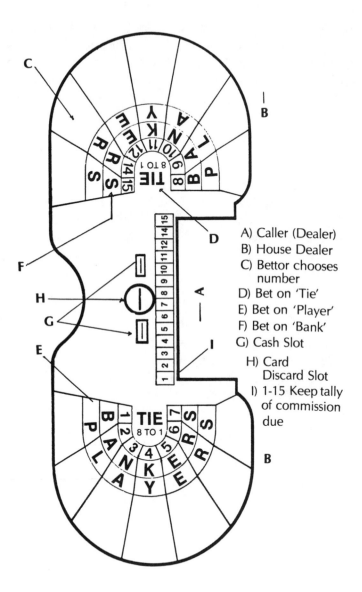

A) Caller (Dealer)
B) House Dealer
C) Bettor chooses
   number
D) Bet on 'Tie'
E) Bet on 'Player'
F) Bet on 'Bank'
G) Cash Slot
H) Card
   Discard Slot
I) 1-15 Keep tally
   of commission
   due

A typical baccarat table layout

Baccarat is played with either six or eight decks of cards, without jokers. The game is played like this: one of the dealers will call out, "Shuffle," and begin to shuffle the cards. Unlike other card games, the shuffle is an elegant maneuver, a practiced interleaving of the cards. When this is completed, a player will be asked to cut the cards with a special yellow card simply called the "cut-card." The decks will then be placed in the shoe, ready for dealing. A dealer will turn up the first card from the shoe, and "burn" the number of cards according to the value of the first card. This simply means he places those cards in the discard tray, where all used cards are dealt, without letting the players see them. For example, if the first card out of the deck is a 3, he will take three cards out of the deck and place them in the discard tray. The shoe is then given to the player seated immediately to the right of the dealer. This player is the "banker." The bank stays with that player until the bank bet loses. It then moves counterclockwise around the table.

There is no advantage or disadvantage in being the banker, it is merely part of the ceremony, a hangover from the older European versions of baccarat in which the holder of the bank has significant advantages. The banker does not have to bet on the bank if he chooses not to.

Players then make their bets, which can be on either player, bank, or tie, or any combination of the three. The "caller" says, "Card for the player," followed by "Card for the banker," then he repeats himself. The first and third cards go to the official "player's hand," which is held by whoever made the largest bet on the player. The second and fourth cards are dealt to the banker. The value of each hand is determined by adding the value of the two cards. Aces count as one, 10s and all face cards count as 0. Suits are not important to the working of the game.

For any total over 9, only the last digit is taken. For example, the 6 of Clubs and 7 of Spades produces a total of 3. The object of the game is to get a total as close to 9 as possible. Now, if either player has an 8 or 9 with their first two cards, it's called a "natural." Eight is commonly called "*le petit*," and 9 "*le grande*." Either one wins outright unless the opposing hand also has a natural. If neither hand has a natural, then we first look at the player hand. If the player holds a score between 0 and 5, the player draws a third card; if the player holds a score of 6 or 7, the player stands. Now look at the banker's hand. With a total from 0 to 2, the banker always draws, with a 3 the bank draws unless the player drew and its third card was an 8. With a 4, the bank draws unless the player drew and its third card was either an 8, 9, or an Ace.

The banker draws on a total of 5 unless the player drew and its third card was outside the range of 4 through 7. With a 6, the bank stands unless the player drew and its third card was either a 6 or a 7. With a 7, the bank stands.

Bank Drawing vs. Player's Draw

Bank Draw Card	N	0	1	2	3	4	5	6	7	8	9	←Player's Card
9	–	–	–	–	–	–	–	–	–	–	–	
8	–	–	–	–	–	–	–	–	–	–	–	
7	–	–	–	–	–	–	–	–	–	–	–	
6	–	–	–	–	–	–	–	D	D	–	–	
5	D	–	–	–	–	D	D	D	D	–	–	
4	D	–	–	D	D	D	D	D	D	–	–	
3	D	D	D	D	D	D	D	D	D	–	D	
2	D	D	D	D	D	D	D	D	D	D	D	
1	D	D	D	D	D	D	D	D	D	D	D	
0	D	D	D	D	D	D	D	D	D	D	D	

D = draw; N = no card drawn by player

It is not necessary to understand these complex rules in order to take part in a game of baccarat. At every point, the caller will instruct the players what to do. It is only important to understand the rules if you wish to know the mathematics of the game, and thereby gain an advantage applying hard-won knowledge.

Baccarat is a community game. All the participants are interested in the outcome of one hand and one hand only, unlike most other card games, where the player faces an adversarial battle against the dealer or another player. Unlike other card games, all the attention of the players on the table is focused on the four, five, or six cards that make up the baccarat hand. This is why onlookers gather to watch high rollers at baccarat, as the spectacle is a ritual that could be designed for easy public viewing. There is something compelling about the tense and deliberate slow turn of each card, upon which may lie the key to riches or ruin. The hearts of the gamblers soar and fall as each hand brings tragedy or euphoria, fascination and foreboding.

After the final value of the player and bank hand is declared, the high hand wins. If the hands are of the same value, a tie is declared, and both the player and banker bets are returned to the players. The payoff for a winning bet on the player is 1 to 1. The banker bet, which has a higher chance of success than the player bet, is paid at 1 to 0.95. This is because the casino takes a commission, or *cagnotte*, of 5 percent for all winning bets on the bank hand. Commissions on the bank hand are recorded by one of the dealers. The amount is usually settled once the shoe has been dealt out or the player leaves the table. Ties are paid off at 8 to 1. Casinos usually advertise this as 9 *for* 1.

Games of chance are run so that a small percentage favors the game operators at the expense of the players. In the short term, luck will shift back and forth between the house and its customers. Over the long term, however, the results will average out to give the house its percentage of every bet placed. Except in very unusual circumstances, the house always plays with this "edge" in its favor. This edge not only accounts for casinos' profits, but must also cover their expenses. Someone has to pay for all those chandeliers.

The best bet is to side with the banker. The banker bet has a house edge of 1.06 percent. This is one of the most favorable bets in the casino. Many players think that because of the commission, the bank is a bad bet. In fact, the bank has a slight informational advantage—the bank's third-card drawing decision is based on a logical assessment of the player hand. For example, it helps the bank to stand on a 3 when the player draws an 8 as his third card. Though normally a bad total, the banker's 3 will beat the player's total 3 to 2 (three out of five) occasions, giving him a substantial edge in this situation. The banker benefits from knowing that the player has probably worsened his hand by drawing an

8. The player's first two cards could total only 0 to 5, so an 8 will help only on 0 or 1 and hinder on 2, 3, 4, or 5. A banker's 3 will beat the player if his two-card score is 3 or 4 ($+8=0$, 1, or 2), lose against a player's two-card 0 or 1 ($+8=8$ or 9), and tie against the player's 5 ($+8=3$).

Most casinos specify a minimum commission charge, for example, $1, so if your bet is low you will be giving the house more than 5 percent commission. In this case, when you are betting $10 and the minimum commission is $1, you are giving 10 percent to the house. If the minimum commission ever exceeds one-twentieth of your bet, the bank is no longer a good bet and you should then side with the player.

Incidentally, the banker's strategy is not the best one. The optimal strategy would be for the banker to draw a holding 4 against a player's Ace, and draw a holding 6 against a player's no-draw.

If you learn nothing else about baccarat, at least know this: it is an amazing fact that by betting on the bank continuously you will have a better chance of winning than 95 percent of all other players! That piece of advice has just turned you into a baccarat expert!

The house tax on the banker is effectively 2.2930 percent per hand. Generally speaking, this amount is not deducted after every hand; the croupier will keep track of the individual banker wins and collect the total at the end of the shoe or when the gamer leaves the table. The 5 percent commission may sometimes be raised to a minimum level, e.g., $1. This would mean that a player who bet less than $20 on the banker would be giving the house more than 5 percent. In this case, it is better for him to bet on the player, as that bet will effectively give a lower house edge.

The player bet gives the house a 1.23 percent advantage. This may not sound like much, and, indeed, compared to most other bets in the casino it is very favorable (as we'll see later), but you should understand that in the long run, this small advantage to the house is decisive. Over a long period of play, the house edge becomes more and more decisive, till the gambler is virtually certain to be behind. To put it in its proper perspective, in baccarat and other casino games this small edge of a little more than 1 percent is responsible for the gilded magnificence of some of the world's grandest casinos. The foundations of the world's great gambling centers, Las Vegas and Monaco, were laid on just such a small edge. In a short period of play, however, it is of comparatively little importance. The tie bet, widely ridiculed as a "sucker bet," has a 14.36 percent edge for the casino. The following chart gives you precise information as to the house edges for various bets and their win probabilities in a typical game:

Number of Decks	Banker Wins	Player Wins	Tie
Infinite	45.84%	44.61%	9.54%
Eight	45.85%	44.62%	9.52%
Six	45.86%	44.62%	9.50%

The house edges are as follows:

Number of Decks	Banker Wins		Player Wins	Tie	
	5% Comm.	4% Comm.		9–1	8–1
Infinite	1.06%	.61%	1.23%	4.54%	14.12%
Eight	1.06%	.60%	1.23%	4.84%	14.36%
Six	1.06%	.60%	1.24%	4.93%	14.44%

(An infinite deck is one which never runs out of cards, or, alternatively, a deck which is shuffled after every card is dealt. No casino would do this; this is for illustrative purposes only, although there is a casino in Las Vegas that once used a 144-deck shoe!)

The reason the house edge is higher for the tie bet, if six decks are used rather than eight, is related to the fact that when six decks are used the removal of a card changes the deck structure more rapidly. This decreases the chances of the player and banker drawing same-valued cards, which greatly increases the chances of a tie when it occurs. To illustrate, say we are playing a game with eight decks and the player draws a 6 for his first card. The chance that the banker will draw a 6 for his first card is 7.46 percent. In a six-deck game, the chance would be 7.39 percent. This difference is relatively slight, but becomes more important as more cards are dealt.

Something similar happens to the player and bank bets, though not to any noticeable degree. The bank bet becomes fractionally more profitable at the expense of the player bet. It is hard to see why this should be the case, but it probably has to do with the fact that the bank's more complicated rules for drawing a third card allow it to compensate for changes from the ordinary deck structure, while the player's "brute force" rules for drawing a third card do not. For a more detailed discussion of the effects of card removal, refer to Chapter 3.

Eliminating ties, the banker wins 50.68 percent of the time, compared to the player's 49.32 percent. If ties are not counted as trials, then the house advantage over the banker should be 1.1692 percent, and over the player 1.3650 percent. In this instance, the house "tax" on the banker is 2.5341 percent. It can be seen that the banker and player are mutually exclusive entities in the tradition of other gambling games, such as red and black at roulette, or the "do" and "don't" bets at craps. Unlike other casino games, however, there is no stigma attached to betting against what the other players at the table are doing. If you sit down and bet banker while everyone else is betting on a player streak, you will not be blamed if the player hand wins. This may come as news to dice players.

The banker bet is unusual in that it is the only bet in the casino which offers less than even money on a winning bet. Most casinos cater to human nature by offering wagers which pay 1 to 1 or greater. The bank bet is the best bet baccarat offers, but because of its 0.95 return on investment it is not as likely as many less favorable wagers to win you a large amount of money on a very lucky streak. For the same reasons, it will not lose you as much money on a long losing streak.

My inquiries into the existence of the tie bet revealed that it had originally been offered at 9 to 1, but over the years it was gradually replaced by the less favorable payoff. I have no idea why this is the case. Possibly greed? A casino in Maryland offered the tie at 9 to 1 as part of a weekend promotion last year, though I believe this has been discontinued. There are probably casinos that offer this elsewhere. I have also been told that lower bank commissions and higher tie payoffs are often granted to high rollers on request.

Why is the tie bet such a bad wager compared to the bank and player bets? For two reasons. First, the gambling industry has long realized that people overvalue long-shot wagers, while simultaneously undervaluing short-odds wagers. By and large, gamblers prefer to risk a small amount of money in the hope of an occasional big payoff than risk a large amount in the virtual certainty of a small payoff. Because of this, you will usually find that long-odds wagers have a very high house take, because the public will tolerate awful odds in the hope of making a big score. This isn't just in baccarat, by the way. In roulette, the even-chance wagers are more favorable than the single numbers; at craps, the *don't pass* and *don't come* bets are vastly more favorable than the field bets; at the races or the dogtrack, you will find you will lose much less betting on hot favorites than on outsiders.

Second, tie bets have a higher "variance" than other bets. This means that runs of luck on the tie are much more extreme than on the bank or player. By way of illustration, consider the possible outcome for a gambler who bets on the player three times, beginning with a $20 stake and parlaying his winnings. On the first hand he wins $20, doubles his bet on the next hand and wins $40, doubles again and wins $80 on the third hand, a total of $140. If he'd been following the same strategy on the tie and had won three times in a row, he'd win $180 on the first bet, $1,600 on the second, and $14,400 on the third, a total of $16,180. Now, this is very unlikely to happen (three ties will occur less than .1 percent of the time) but it is possible, and so sooner or later it will happen to some lucky player. Should a player take a chance on extremely good fortune, the consequences for the casino are much more damaging. To protect itself, it compensates for the higher risk by offering worse odds.

Players who wish to mix up their bets should know that a bet on the banker and tie simultaneously has a 55.4 percent chance of winning, while player and tie win 54.2 percent of the time. Betting banker *and* player is too impractical to be given any consideration, as it would result in no change to your bankroll if the player wins, or a loss of 5 percent of your wager if the bank wins. Be aware that mixing your bets has no effect on the expectations of any of the bets, that is, betting player and tie on one hand is identical to betting player on one hand and tie on the next. You will, however, lose faster if you bet on more than one event simultaneously. Betting the tie will put a serious drain on the comparatively favorable bank and player wagers. I would therefore treat the tie exactly as it is—a side bet. If you bet $100 on the banker and $20 on the tie, your expectation is 3.2 percent or 3.3 percent if you bet on the player and the tie. Some would consider this a small amount given that it provides you with a good chance of winning the hand, though I would not recommend this style of betting for protracted play.

Table Minimums and Maximums

A casino typically will require you to bet at least $20 in order to participate in a game of big table baccarat. The maximum may be as little as $1,000 in a real "sawdust" joint, to $20,000 in some of the larger Las Vegas casinos, many of whom will have baccarat pits cordoned off for the purpose of catering to the player who wishes to bet at this level.

Whatever the signposted limit is, players can usually make special arrangements to go much higher than this. It's not unheard of for a player to negotiate a $200,000 maximum. From the casino's perspective, the more that is bet the more money they make, but they must also be careful that a fantastic run of good luck for a player does not wipe out their resources (this does happen occasionally). Sometimes groups of highly-paid executives will monopolize a table and all bet on one side. Since they are all betting on the same hand, the casino is effectively running the same risk as if one player was betting the total amount.

To give you an idea of the expected wins and losses casino staff expect, you might be surprised to find that a player winning $250,000 barely raises an eyelid in most of the Las Vegas Strip casinos. Most casino managers instruct their staff to contact them only if a player is winning $1 million or more.

Dress Codes

Despite the image of baccarat as a game in which the players are immaculately attired in the finest clothing, most casinos in the United States are not so fussy. As Jack Binion (owner of Binion's Horseshoe) said, "If you walk into our pit with a cool twenty-five grand, our baccarat manager will determine that you meet our dress code just fine." Nevertheless, players generally do dress smartly in order not to seem out of place in the luxury of the surroundings—but don't be intimidated. This is the twentieth century, after all. If you don't want to wear a suit, let alone a tuxedo, don't.

Most of the rules and rituals of baccarat are identical everywhere in the world, except that the game is sometimes called Punto Banco, when the three bets are referred to as *punto, banco,* and *egalite* instead of player, bank, and tie. Undoubtedly, the best place in the world to play baccarat, and in many ways its spiritual home, is the French Riviera. There, it's still possible to wander into a plush casino to see baccarat conducted with the grace and elegance of a string quartet playing Vivaldi.

Baccarat is also played in England, the Philippines, Malaysia, Spain, South Africa, Egypt, South Korea, and the larger countries of Eastern Europe.

European Punto Banco vs. American Baccarat

Americans who play Punto Banco in Europe typically experience a certain amount of culture shock. The admittance procedures are awkward, usually requiring identification and sometimes advance arrangements. The casinos usually open and close on a rather arbitrary basis. American casinos will go to extravagant lengths to court high rollers; in Europe, overt attempts to attract such patrons are absent, and there are usually no free inducements to play except the occasional cocktail or sandwich. The casinos are smaller, and they are less noisy than their American counterparts, owing to the comparative unimportance of slot machines. Punto Banco is better suited to the ambiance of Europe.

Be aware that the aristocracy in Europe, who still run large elements of the casino industry, particularly in countries with a strong aristocratic tradition (including both royalist Britain and republican France), have a very elitist, almost snobbish attitude toward membership criteria. In some cases, there is a state of mind toward the American player that borders on the xenophobic.

Money is not the only thing that counts in Europe; taste and good manners are also important (no bad thing in itself). Extravagant displays of wealth are frowned upon. A large amount of money will not guarantee entry into a high-society establishment. Dress codes are stricter, though this is changing. Usually smart casual clothing is the norm, except for the most plushly carpeted establishments.

This is particularly the case in the capital cities of Europe. The provincial areas are generally more laid-back and cater to the local and less wealthy punter. Because of this, you will not find any baccarat in the smaller towns, as the regulars could not afford to play it.

Players should be aware that European players are much less vocal than their American counterparts in reacting to turns of fate. An exasperated *"Mon Dieu"* is about as heated as it gets. What might be regarded as acceptable emotional expression in the United States might get you permanently barred from the tables. Nevertheless, if you are serious about the game, you must really play where it is meant to be played, in its spiritual home.

How to Play Mini-Baccarat

Mini-baccarat is a game more suited to the casual gambler. It was introduced largely to appeal to ordinary gamblers who felt intimidated by the main version of the game. Mathematically, it is exactly the same as its big-table cousin, but without the ceremony and with a generally friendlier atmosphere. The game is played on a blackjack-size table with seven player spots and a solitary dealer. Each player spot has two circles in front of him, one marked "player" the other "banker."

Above this is a semicircular strip which runs along the table, marked "tie" at both ends, and divided into numbered areas which correspond to the players' positions at the table. Eight or six decks of cards are used. All the chips are kept in a tray directly in front of the dealer. In front of this is a box where commissions on the bank hand are recorded.

The dealer does all of the shuffling, a player selected by the dealer cuts the cards when the shuffle has been completed, and the cut decks are put in the shoe. As with the big-table game, practices vary, but a common method of determining how many cards will be dealt is to turn one card face up and burn a number of cards equal to the value of that card. Then the players make their bets and the game begins. The dealer will give the first and third card to his right (the player hand) and the second and fourth card to his left (the banker hand). The rules are identical to those of big-table baccarat.

Mini-baccarat usually has much lower table minimums, typically as little as $5, but the quite reasonable house edge of baccarat proper is normally maintained. The game is currently offered exclusively in the United States, as other countries with legalized gambling tend to derive more of their profits from high rollers than large numbers of ordinary players. The game, however, has become very successful in the United States. In Mississippi, for example, it has almost completely displaced big-table baccarat.

Shuffling Machines

New machines that shuffle cards automatically have recently been introduced on an experimental basis at mini-baccarat in some casinos. When the pack of cards has been dealt, the dealer gathers up the discards and places them inside the machine, where they are shuffled more thoroughly and more quickly than any human dealer could manage. Casinos hire these devices to get more hands dealt per hour by reducing shuffling time. The more hands that are dealt, the more money they make, and the less risk they run. Also, players tend to leave the game during a shuffle. The faster the shuffle, it is less likely players will leave.

The devices do not affect the odds of the game in any way. Players are naturally suspicious of the machines, believing they may be programmed to help the house in some way. It is difficult to see how this could be achieved. In fact, it is more likely that the thorough shuffling creates a game that is more random, and therefore more "honest," than a human shuffle could.

The devices do not appear to be particularly well designed; frequently they jam, and sometimes they break down altogether. The dealers generally hate them, perhaps because they feel they are being replaced. The machines can also ruin the atmosphere. If you do not like playing with a shuffling machine, vote with your wallet and go elsewhere; there are plenty of casinos that do not use them.

Promotions

The Horseshoe, in Las Vegas, was among a number of casinos which have recently been offering a 4 percent commission. Authors such as Victor H. Royer have stated (without reference to any specific casino) that 3 percent commissions are sometimes offered. Frankly, I doubt it. The banker bet would have an average advantage of only 0.16 percent. This is so small as to be hardly worth the casino's while in offering the bet. Nevertheless, the Sahara Sands in Las Vegas went even further than this in 1996 and did away with the commission altogether! Unfortunately, this was only during a very brief promotion. For the lucky players who chanced on it, however, they had 1.23 percent advantage every time they bet on the bank.

A few years back, there were several casinos in Hong Kong, Macao, and Sri Lanka, before the most recent violence there, which offered "happy hours," with no bank commission, on a regular basis. If you should ever find a casino offering reduced or no commission, the table below will help you find out its value. Generally, anything less than 4 percent becomes very appealing from the player's point of view, but it is only likely to exist as a short-term promotion.

Why do casinos offer promotions? Largely as a loss leader, to attract new customers and reward regular players. In truth, the casino doesn't lose much when it does offer a promotion, because most players, rather than sticking all their money on the bank as the math would dictate, follow trending systems which dilute their advantage with unfavorable bets on the player or tie.

Commission	House Edge on bank
6%	−1.52%
3%	−0.15%
2%	0.31%
1%	0.77%
No commission	1.23%

The 6 percent commission is a rule enforced by some Far Eastern casinos. Do not play any such game, as this will only encourage the greed of casino owners everywhere. If you do, however, bet on the player as much as you can. If you ever find a no-commission game, it can be very valuable; 1.23 percent might not sound like much, but this is equivalent to the house's advantage with the player bet. This will allow you to play with a larger advantage than many professional poker and blackjack players, and you will not have to perform the mental gymnastics necessary to win at these games. You will also be able to win more money than you would at any other game in which you have an advantage because the bank bet has a very low variance. This means that you will not get streaks as wild as you would in poker or blackjack, chiefly because in baccarat you do not have to put up any more money than your initial stake. Therefore, you can bet much larger amounts in baccarat than you could at other games with the same advantage.

Betting Strategy in No-Commission Games

To most players, the difference between the house having a 1 percent advantage over you, and you having a 1 percent over the house, might not seem like much. To illustrate the difference this makes, take the example of a player who has $2,000 and bets $20 per hand on the bank in a no-commission game. He has a greater than 90 percent chance of doubling his money before losing it. Note that this is the exact reverse of the ordinary situation, in which the bank gets a 5 percent commission. When the odds are against you, the best tactic is to shove out as much money as possible. When they are with you, you want to employ the opposite strategy, betting conservatively till your long-run advantage kicks in.

The correct way to bet in a no-commission game is simple: bet 1 percent of your "bankroll" on each and every hand. Your bankroll is the amount of money you're willing to risk gambling, and should be separated from the money you need for necessities. Of course, it's not practical to reassess your bet on every hand, but you should reassess your bet every time you take a break or if your bankroll rises or falls dramatically. A good strategy is to cut your bets in half when your bankroll is halved, and to double your bets when your bankroll is doubled. This will allow you to win at the fastest rate possible without running an unacceptable risk of going broke.

For more information on correct betting strategy, see Appendix D.

Do I Have to Bet Every Hand?

Neither in big-table nor mini-baccarat is it necessary to bet on every hand. The house knows that a lot of players like to wait for certain win-loss patterns to occur before placing a bet. Some casinos will continue dealing regardless of whether or not there is a wager on the table.

The speed of the game varies greatly according to the number of players at the table and the habits of the players. Many players enjoy heightening the tension of the game by turning their cards over with great deliberation. On average, big-table baccarat is by far the slowest of all casino table games. Mini-baccarat is another story, however, and as many as six hundred hands can be dealt in an hour. Even playing alone, you would rarely get through eight decks in much less than an hour at the big game.

Tipping

In both versions of baccarat it is customary to tip, or "toke," the dealer(s) when you leave the table or after a series of big wins. How much is up to you. Generally, the table minimum is the least you can get away with, but don't tip if you feel the dealer has been in any way discourteous or intimidating, or appears to enjoy seeing players lose. If you have received good service, however, it is in your interest to encourage the service to continue at the same high standard.

The casino personnel understand that you are less likely to tip after a losing session. By the same token, the dealers expect you to tip heavily after a big win. Personally, I don't agree with this logic. My money is my money. The game is the game. Unless the dealers are cheating the house for my benefit, they should have no say in whether I win or whether I lose. My sole criterion for tipping is to do so when the casino personnel have made my gambling more enjoyable.

The dealers derive a large part of their income from tips. Tipping is pretty much customary the world over. The exception is in England, where tipping is forbidden by law. In other parts of Europe, such as Germany, dealers may not receive a salary and derive their sole income from tips. In these countries you may find that if you do not tip generously the dealers will simply get up and leave the table.

Tipping, in effect, adds to the house edge against you. Tipping a few average-size bets every hour will double the casino advantage and jeopardize your bankroll. Because of this, you should be very wary of overtipping. In the larger casinos, don't worry about it too much; dealers in the baccarat pit are usually pretty well paid.

Is Baccarat a Good Deal?

Either version of baccarat offers some of the best odds in the casino. Craps is the only game to offer a straight-up bet with a better bet—the line bet with odds has a house edge of just 0.8 percent. However, the field, proposition, and other bets have advantages of between 1.5 to 16.7 percent. The 1.06 percent baccarat bank bet also measures up nicely against the 5.4 percent edge on double-zero roulette (2.7 percent with single-zero, 1.35 percent on even chances with the much more favorable European *en prison* rule). The relatively new games of Red Dog or Acey-Deucey has a comparatively low house edge, at 2.36 percent, while the popular poker-based Let It Ride is higher, at 3.5 percent. Both these games require you to play the best strategy even to lose at this rate. Other forms of casino gambling do not even come close to baccarat. The dice game of Chuck-a-Luck is strictly for suckers only, with house edges ranging from 3 to 8 percent on its various wagers. *The Wheel of Fortune*, or *Big Six*, has a very prohibitive 18 percent take, while keno, the loser's game par excellence, has a lottery-style 25 percent edge. Slot machines, which have become the casinos' bread-and-butter in recent years, can have a house edge of close to break-even or a fraudulent 20 percent, depending on casino policy and the value of the coin required for play.

On every wager, blackjack players are estimated to earn, on average, 2 percent for the house. Although skilled players can actually turn the odds in their favor, there are very few who are sufficiently talented, patient, and disciplined to actually do this on a regular basis. (In fact, the true professional can turn almost any casino game to his advantage, but that's another story.)

Baccarat clearly provides the best combination of simplicity and favorable odds in the casino. If you ignore the tie bet, then the game is by far the casino's best value. Unfortunately, the majority of ordinary players ignore the grand game and head straight for the slots. It's partly because of the intimidating and secluded atmosphere that surrounds the big table, but many people are also put off by the complicated drawing-and-standing rules and the peculiar scoring system, which is silly considering that it really doesn't make any difference whether you understand them or not. You'll often wander past a luxurious baccarat pit set with crystal chandeliers and find a string of empty tables. Don't walk by; this is a golden opportunity to learn the game. You can only get so much from a book; experience the thrill of baccarat first hand.

2

The History of Baccarat

Baccarat (literally meaning "zero") was first played in Italy during the fourteenth century, though its origin stretches back almost indefinitely into prehistory. Richard Epstein, writing in *The Theory of Gambling and Statistical Logic,* traced the game to a Roman legend written long before the birth of Christ. The legend tells of a young vestal virgin whose fate was to be decided by the gods. She was to throw a *novem dare,* or nine-sided die. If she rolled an 8 or 9, she was to become a high priestess. If she rolled a 6 or 7, she was to be disqualified from religious office and her vestal status discontinued. Anything less and she was to walk into the sea, never to return.

Structurally, baccarat is descended from a Chinese game called Pai Gow, a tile game. Pai Gow literally means "to make nine"—the object of baccarat—and shares modulo ten arithmetic and shifting bank option with the Italian game. The game may have been introduced into Italy via the explorations of Marco Polo.

Two derivations of the game subsequently evolved—*baccarat en Banque*, and with the spread of the game into France during the reign of Charles VIII, a version now called chemin de fer.

At first it was an illegal game, but after a while baccarat was legalized and a tax was imposed on it which was donated to the welfare of the underprivileged. Upon legalization, the game soared in popularity across France. The connection with charity proved to be a masterstroke, as it helped clear the people's natural association between gambling and decadence—they could now be conscientious gamblers.

The game would fall out of fashion in years to come, and as quickly and mysteriously it would return. During the reign of Napoleon it was unfashionable, and later, at the time of Louis-Philippe, the "People's King," it was banned altogether, and remained so from 1837 to 1907, when all gambling in France was declared illegal. Nevertheless, it thrived in the underworld. As it was played then, the game was very much a staple of cardsharps and cheats, and without official approval the cheated player had little redress.

Late in the nineteenth century, these games became staples of the casinos across Europe, especially France and Monte Carlo. Syndicates would form to hold the bank, and baccarat became the game of choice among the rich, as it acquired a reputation for European sophistication. The game also became popular among the English aristocracy, most notably under the stewardship of John Aspinall's private games and at the famous Crockford's club in London.

Trente et quarante is a French card game, the object of which is to achieve a total close to 31. Scarney Baccarat and Quick-Draw Baccarat were unsuccessful attempts to mix the best elements of blackjack and baccarat. Both games are no longer available in the casinos. The other games are given full descriptions in later chapters.

In 1890, the game reached its highest level of importance when it shook the foundations of the British Empire in what is now referred to as the Royal Baccarat Scandal, a fascinating and true tale. The affair concerned the bachelor and philanderer Sir William Gordon-Cumming, a personal friend of the Prince of Wales, with whom he played the then illegal game of baccarat at many country house parties. On one evening in the 1890s, at the home of a shipping millionaire, five of the players accused Gordon-Cumming of manipulating the stakes at the gaming table, and he was threatened with public exposure. In order to protect the prince's reputation, he signed an agreement never to play baccarat again. The prince refused to defend his lifelong companion,

Genealogy of Baccarat

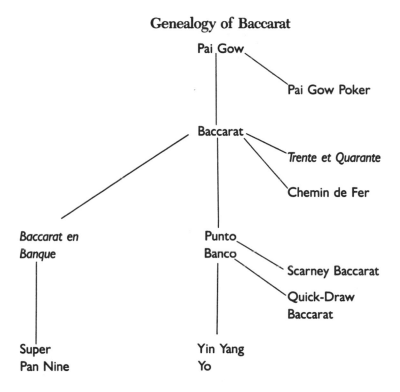

and Gordon-Cumming was banished from the royal circle. Bitter at this betrayal of trust, Gordon-Cumming launched a lawsuit in order to clear his name, but despite serious irregularities in the evidence, he was defeated and disgraced. Due to his high living, the prince remained popular with the masses, but the affair seriously tested the patience of his mother, Queen Victoria, and the British establishment.

When gambling was again legalized in France in 1907, baccarat regained its former popularity. Beautiful casinos were built throughout the country in which the game enjoyed pride of place. Notable casinos exist to this day in Nice, Cannes, Biarritz, Deauville, and, of course, neighboring Monaco.

Baccarat remained popular among the aristocracy, and the first primitive attempts to analyze the game were made by a number of French mathematicians. Syndicates began to form to hold the bank in that country in the different forms of baccarat, as it became apparent that much money was to be made from absorbing the wealth of nouveau riche playboy aristocrats. By the 1920s, a team formed at Deauville calling itself the Greek Syndicate, led by Nico Zographos, arguably the most successful freelance professional gambler of all time. They were to dominate the high-stakes gambling scene in Monte Carlo, Cannes, and Deauville for the next few decades, their iron grip broken only temporarily by the outbreak of World War II. The syndicate accepted challenges from all comers, like the bank in *baccarat en banque*. They were a five-man partnership, also composed of an Armenian and a Frenchman, despite the syndicate's name. The syndicate played a version of *baccarat en banque* entitled *à tout va,* meaning they played without limits. The wealthy came from every corner of the globe with the ambition of breaking the syndicate. Its success was largely due to Zographos. An Athens-born former engineer, he was one of the first gamblers to apply scientific methods to gambling.

With Zographos's skill, the Greek Syndicate prospered for more than thirty years; he was capable of memorizing an entire deck of cards, and, at the same time, developed an unparalleled ability to read his opponent's body language. The methods Zographos used are indicative of a prototype card-counting system (see Chapter 3) combined with what is now known as "tell-play" (see Chapter 8). Both methods were not widely understood or explained until long after Zographos's death, in 1953. Zographos left the greatest fortune ever amassed from card playing, equivalent to some $5 million at the time. He once bet one million francs on one hand, when the syndicate's funds were dangerously close to extinction.

On the first deal he received a zero-valued card (the worst card to begin with), the second was the 9 of Diamonds, making a total of 9, a perfect natural. The hand broke the losing streak against the syndicate, and Zographos put the 9 of Diamonds on the pennant on his yacht. By comparison, consider that the great blackjack players Lawrence Revere and Ken Uston each won only about $1 million during their lifetimes, and there was substantial inflation in the years separating their eras from that of the Greek Syndicate. Following Zographos's death, the syndicate floundered and was eventually broken in 1957, as two Hollywood film producers, Jack Warner and Darryl Zanuck, with an Englishman, Bob Barnett, won $347,000 when the syndicate lost more than $800,000 in a few days play. An analysis of the last few hands which led to the syndicate's demise suggests that the syndicate banker was seriously lacking in elementary knowledge of the probabilities of the game. With the end of the syndicate, the popularity of high-stakes betting faded for a time; but the syndicate had given, as its legacy to the game that had both made and ruined it, the mystique upon which its allure depends.

In the 1950s, the center of the gambling world abruptly shifted to Las Vegas. Tentative attempts were made to introduce chemin de fer, without success. Las Vegas glitz and European elegance proved incompatible.

Nevertheless, a version of the game evolved called *Punto y Banca*. This was first introduced at the famous Mar del Plata casino, in Argentina. The game spread through Latin America to pre-communist Cuba, where it attracted the attention of one Tommy Renzoni, the man responsible for bringing the game from Havana to the Dunes Casino in Las Vegas, in 1959. On the first night the game was introduced the players used cash, and the owners found themselves with a profitable new avenue of gaming revenue on their hands. Renzoni never received credit for introducing the game and remained a casino employee of modest income compared to the players his brainchild attracted. After failed attempts to introduce further game innovations into Vegas and the death of his wife, Renzoni became disillusioned with life. One day he simply walked blindly into the middle of a street and took his own life. His legacy, Punto Banco, gradually replaced the older versions of baccarat.

This is the modern form of the game. Americans now simply call the game baccarat, or sometimes baccarat chemin de fer. It differs from the European forms of the game in that the house banks all the bets, the players may bet on a tie or the bank hand, and standing-and-drawing decisions are not permitted. It is purely a mechanical game.

Progression Systems and Why They Don't Work

There are a number of systems that have been devised for baccarat that appear to work. Often they are available through mail order at inflated prices. The ads will tell you how you can live a life of luxury if you buy their easy-to-use system. In gambling circles, the phrase used to describe such systems is "snake oil," after the con men who lived in the Old West selling their worthless potion as a cure-all to a society ignorant of medical science. Most of the systems involve some sort of progressive betting. They can be all be used on either bank (although the 19-20 makes things a little awkward) or player bets, but not the tie, as the 8 to 1 payoff complicates matters. Most of the older systems were originally designed for roulette. I will examine a few, some of which you may have heard about:

The Martingale

This is the oldest and simplest system (though it is often misnamed "martindale"). It was first devised in the sixteenth century by the mad Polish inventor Joseph Wronski. Thousands of people rediscover it each year, as it is a very seductive system.

The player doubles his bet every time he loses. If the table minimum is $20, a Martingale sequence would go like this: $20, $40, $80, $160, $320, $640, $1280.... You can see that if you win at any point you would be $20 ahead. In theory, you could keep on doubling your bet and never lose. This would, however, only be true if you had infinite capital, as well as infinite time. The Martingale bettor will almost certainly win in the short term. This convinces a lot of players that it works. In fact, all they are doing is giving themselves a good chance of a small win offset by a small chance of a large loss. Six losses will take you beyond many table maximums.

The anti-Martingale is a system in which the opposite strategy is played. You double your bet every time you win, and reset it to the amount of your first bet when you lose. Consequently, you have a large chance of a small loss and a small chance of a large win.

There are numerous other variations on this most popular of betting systems. Without exception, they have no effect on the long-term odds of the game. In the short term, however, they can have a significant effect. A player who uses the Martingale is certain to walk away from the tables a winner, provided he does not encounter a streak of sufficient length to wipe out his bankroll, but when this does happen, the loss is so great that it counterbalances the series of small wins the bettor is enjoying. In effect, the gambler is trading a small chance of a great loss for a large chance of a small win. If he wishes to win a very small amount, he is likely to do it, but if he plays the Martingale system for any length of time, total ruin is inevitable. A Martingale bettor should expect to win his initial bankroll 50 percent of the time (minus the house edge), before encountering a streak of sufficient length to wipe him out.

Contrary to popular belief, table maximums don't prevent Martingales from working, nor, for that matter, any other progression system. If you encounter a streak of sufficient length to take you above the table maximum of the casino you are playing, you can simply go to a casino with a higher maximum. Binion's Horseshoe has stated publicly that it will accept a bet of pretty much any size. No-limit games can still be found in Monte Carlo, and many casinos will go significantly higher than the table maximum with a little negotiation, especially once they have established that you are using a Martingale system. You can get a friend or friends to bet your money for you on another spot, which is a cunning way of betting above the table maximums without changing the odds. Of course, if your losing streak becomes sufficiently long that you have to start betting in the trillions, no one will accept your bet, as the amount of money in the world is limited.

It's not necessary to go to such extremes, though. If a syndicate could form with a capital of $6 billion, they could send out a player to use the Martingale system at baccarat, preferably betting on the bank on every hand, and be reasonably sure that the syndicate would never even come close to losing its total capital during the natural life span of its members (be thankful I'm not inflicting the math on you here). The return on investment, though, would be absolutely paltry in percentage terms, and, in fact, the syndicate would lose money, as its winnings would be more than outstripped by inflation.

Consider, also, that there is no such thing as a limit to a streak. It's not impossible for the player or bank hand to win ten thousand hands in a row. It's fantastically unlikely, and will probably never occur during the life of the human race, but it *is* possible.

The d'Alembert

This was devised by Jean d'Alembert for use in the private roulette games offered in eighteenth-century France. Such games offered the player a 50 percent wager, as they had no zeros, as in modern American roulette. Because of this, d'Alembert's system made him a fortune. D'Alembert argued that "nature seeks equilibrium," and his system is designed to exploit this. The d'Alembert is additive, where the Martingale is multiplicative. The bettor simply adds one to his bet for a loss and subtracts one for a win. It does not offer the almost certain short-term win that the Martingale does, but there is also no dramatic escalation in bet size that causes many Martingale bettors to be wiped out in a single session.

Unfortunately, nature does not seek equilibrium when the laws of the game are unbalanced, as is the case with the small house edge at baccarat.

The Fibonacci

This system is named for Leonardo Fibonacci of Pisa, a thirteenth-century mathematician whose Liber Abaci was one of the most influential textbooks on arithmetic of that period. The system originates from Fibonacci's famous puzzle: how many pairs of rabbits will be produced each month, beginning with a single pair, if every month each productive pair bears a new pair which becomes productive for the second month and so on. The answer is: 1, 1, 2, 3, 5, 8, 13, 21..., i.e., the number of pairs produced per month is the sum of the pairs produced in the two preceding months. At some unknown point in time, a gambler observed that if this sequence were applied to a series of bets, he could generate a profit with just two successive wins, regardless of what happened previously. It quickly became a popular system and passed into gambling folklore.

The Labouchere (or "cancellation" system)

Of indeterminate origin, this system is any series of numbers that adds up to the total win target the gambler desires. The first and last in the series becomes the initial bet. If the bets win, the numbers are canceled, and the bettor works inward through the series until all the numbers have been canceled, at which point the target win has been obtained. If the bet loses, its value is added to the series, which has to be canceled before the bettor progresses inwards. One number is added to the series if the bet loses, while two numbers are canceled after a win. Therefore, it seems that the Labouchere system offers a 2 to 1 proposition on a 1 to 1 bet.

The Labouchere, d'Alembert and Fibonacci systems all operate on the same principles, but because the bet escalation is not so rapid, the gambler is likely to last longer, though at the cost of being less likely to win as much on a favorable streak. By contrast, systems such as the anti-Martingale effectively trade a large chance of a small loss for the small chance of a great win. This more aggressive approach is ideal for the player who doesn't mind losing small amounts, and every now and then will score a spectacular coup.

By all means, invent your own betting systems. They can be great fun. Then you can gamble in a style which most suits your character. Besides, it's fun to personalize your gambling. Just don't ever fool yourself into thinking you have discovered a winning system. Richard Epstein's *Theory of Gambling and Statistical Logic* contains a complicated technical explanation of the fallacious nature of betting systems. Every gambler would do well to remember Epstein's first theorem: "An unfavorable game remains unfavorable regardless of the variation in bets."

Streaks

Most literature on baccarat talks about streaks. Casinos encourage players to record the results of streaks by providing tally sheets and pens. Would they do this if they thought it helped you win money from them? No!

The most popular streaking system is known as the Avant Dernier.

The idea behind this system is simple: you simply bet on the outcome of the sequence which showed up two times before last, so a sequence of hands which went banker, player, banker, player, player would tell you to bet on the player.

There are many other trending systems. Sometimes they are called "hot," "cold," or "impatient," styles of betting, where a gambler either waits for a sequence of hands favoring the player or banker and bets the opposite, while the other involves waiting for such a sequence to occur and sticking with the trend. These systems have their origin in a misunderstanding of the law of averages.

Players who follow streaks do so on the assumption that a sequence of wins for the bank, player, or tie means that streak is more likely than not to continue. In fact, after a win by the bank, player, or tie, the subsequent chance of this bet winning again is *less* likely, though by such a small fraction of a percent that most modern computers are incapable of calculating it. For all practical purposes, there is no relation between the result of one hand and the next. Buying into streaks, betting either for or against them, only increases your chances of losing, as gaining the best chance of winning all your bets should be with the banker. This may come as a surprise to experienced baccarat players. It may seem strange that simply continuously betting on the bank is superior to any other strategy, but this is undeniably the case. If you attempt to ride streaks or follow trends, your expectation will be an average of the three bets, which will give you greater losses in the long run.

Gambling "authorities," such as John Patrick in his series of gambling books, continue to advocate the use of trending techniques. Some shoes are apparently player-biased, some are bank-biased, some are tie-biased, and some are, intriguingly, not biased at all. Unfortunately, there is no way of knowing if a shoe will remain with the bias (if any) it started with, or if it will behave completely differently. Streaks only arrive after the event and are completely useless for predicting future events. There is no truth at all in the popular misconception that "baccarat is a game of streaks." If you were to purchase a book on geography which told you the earth was flat, you might feel cheated. Nevertheless, this is no less absurd than the advice offered by many writers who claim expert knowledge of gambling, yet do not appear to understand the law of independent trials.

Streak players have developed their own interesting array of special terms. A streak of six banker wins is called a "dragon," while a shoe of alternating bank and player wins is called "choppy," or a "Ping-Pong." Two consecutive bank or player wins is known as a "pair."

It's human nature to try to make sense of our environment. Unfortunately, this leads the gambler to detect patterns where none exist. It's just like seeing faces in the clouds.

Take the example of a ten-hand series of wins for the banker. On average, this will occur once every 512 hands. Sometimes it will occur more frequently, sometimes less. If you play 512 hands you might well get a ten-hand streak three or four times. Then you might think you could buy into a series of bank wins in the future and make a big profit. The next series of 512 hands, however, just might contain no ten-hand runs at all, and things will have evened out, while you have lost your money.

Forgetting for a moment the important question of card-counting, the best strategy for a player depends on what he is trying to achieve. In a sense, it is irrational to play baccarat, or any other casino game, as the player would have a higher expectation by not playing at all. If a player wants to win a small amount, he should use a system such as the d'Alembert, which gives a good chance of winning over a session or two, without too much risk. For the best chance of success, the gambler should always bet on the bank, regardless of the system he uses.

The Packer Method

During Christmas 1996, Kerry Packer and ten Asian acquaintances descended on Las Vegas. Shortly afterward, the group walked away with $22 million. They were credited with contributing to a 19 percent drop in quarterly profits at the Hilton Hotel Corporation, resulting in shares dropping 11 cents. They did it by playing $250,000 baccarat hands. After draining the Hilton, Packer and his associates moved on to the Mirage casino and came away with another $2 million.

Packer, an Australian media baron who owns a share of casinos in

Sydney and Melbourne, is a celebrated gambler. How did he do it? Has he discovered the secret of winning baccarat? No, not really. Packer's win, while huge by the standards of ordinary gamblers, is unsurprising considering the stakes he plays for. While the casinos have the advantage when they play against him, even their resources are dwarfed by his own. Packer's personal fortune is estimated at $15 billion, which guarantees him an instant line of credit at any casino. As one Las Vegas boss who has refused to allow Packer to play put it, "If you let him dictate the terms, you are gambling like any other sucker—but for millions invested by stockholder's against a billionaire's pocket money."

Packer's technique is to bet high for short periods of perhaps two to three hours over several days, in contrast to the marathon sessions favored by most big spenders. The moment he edges ahead he quits. This is crucial to his success. If a player chains himself to the tables, the casino will eventually grind him down; but a player is likely to have runs of luck in the short term, and is virtually certain to be winning *at some point*. Packer's limitless resources mean there is no possibility of him being ruined by an adverse streak of bad luck.

Unfortunately for him, Packer's winnings are small when contrasted to his total wealth. It would be the equivalent of you or me going into a casino and walking out with $10 or $20. You can, nevertheless, borrow elements of Packer's successful strategy. Never overbet your bankroll, and do not play for long periods. That way you will limit your losses and likely stay a winner in the short term. Of course, to make real money in baccarat we have to use something altogether more potent.

Incidentally, should you ever spot a whale such as Packer dropping a fortune, you have a rare and very valuable opportunity to beat the system—not at baccarat, however, but at the only serious gambling game on earth whose stakes exceed that of baccarat—the stock market. If the amounts lost by a high roller are significant compared to the total wealth of the casino chain, the value of the company will soar and you will have an opportunity to invest in the organization before this becomes common knowledge. Note: this is not insider trading; it's perfectly legal and ethical. It also gives you the great satisfaction of making money out of a millionaire's bad luck.

How Much Is the Player Likely to Lose?

How much money should you take with you to the casino? Too many chips are impractical and provide too much temptation. Too little and you might run out of money with embarrassing haste if the game goes against you, and the chance of a wipeout is naturally increased the less you bring. A simple method to determine how much to bring to an individual session of baccarat is given below:

Determine how many hands you want to play, and what you will bet on average per hand. So, in a session of five hundred hands, with a typical bet on the banker of $10, the player should expect to lose:

0.0106 (the house edge) × $10 (average bet) × 500 (number of hands)
$$= \$53$$

Note: this doesn't mean the player will always lose exactly $53 after five hundred hands. That's just the most likely single outcome. If you add up all the other possible outcomes you'll find that it's very unlikely to occur. Your actual results will usually be just above or just below this figure.

Standard deviation on a single banker bet is 93 cents on each $1 wagered. You can get your overall session fluctuation by multiplying this ratio by the bet and the square root of the number of hands.

The square root of 500 is 22.
0.93 × $10 × 22 = $204—your overall fluctuation.

With this figure you can work out how many chips to buy. By multiplying your overall fluctuation by 3 and adding your expected loss, you get the amount of money you will lose, less than 5 percent of the time during your session—in this case $656. So, capital of $700 would be more than adequate funds for your session.

The Strategy of Maximum Boldness

For the player who wishes to win a certain amount of money, the best method is known as the "strategy of maximum boldness."

Mathematicians and game theorists universally agree that this is the best strategy for a negative expectation game. It works on this principle: the longer a player stays at the baccarat table, the more certain it is that he loses the mathematically expected amount determined by the odds. For example, after a few hands the player could well be ahead or behind. After one hundred thousand hands the odds against him being ahead are astronomical. The best technique is to bet the amount of money you intend to risk during the whole of your life, your goal, *at baccarat or any form of gambling,* on one hand. For one hand, the house advantage is of little importance; luck plays an important part. Note: if you bet on the bank, as you should, then you would have a greater than 50 percent chance of winning. There is a secret bet that a skilled baccarat player can make which will actually give him an advantage in this situation (see Chapter 3). Several gamblers have tried this, betting hundreds of thousands of dollars, and won.

This may seem like crazy logic, but it is unquestionably the best way to bet in a game where the odds are against you, and it's not just my recommendation, but the recommendation of the some of the most talented statisticians, game theorists, and mathematicians in the world.

Of course, many players might consider that it's worthwhile betting at lower levels in order to enjoy their gambling over a longer period of time, since this strategy doesn't take into consideration the pleasure of gambling itself. On the other hand, if you wish to last a little longer at the tables, you will pay a high price in terms of your opportunity to win any money. The player who goes into the casino with $2,000 and bets $5 on bank every hand has only a 10 percent chance of doubling his bankroll, i.e., turning that $2,000 into $4,000, before he goes broke. This represents a chance of going broke that has increased by more than 40 percent from the "maximum boldness" strategy.

How to Win at Every Casino in Las Vegas

The key to this strategy depends on the ambiguity of the word "win." Technically, every player who is ahead of the casino by $1 dollar is winning. Therefore, to claim victory over every casino in Vegas (or Atlantic City, Monte Carlo, or London) all you have to do is win your first bet in each casino. A player usually has a greater than 99 percent chance of being ahead of the casino *at some point,* assuming he has a reasonable bankroll and avoids placing too much money on the tie bet. Obviously, your betting strategy will be important as well. To maximize your chances of achieving your goal, each bet you place should be for the amount that gives you a slight advantage over the casino: If the table minimum is $20, then bet $20; if you lose, bet $21; if you lose, bet $42, and so on. If you restrict yourself to the table minimum at all times you will have slightly less chance of ever being ahead of the casino, but you will not lose so much money on a very unfavorable streak.

The more you do this the more your chances of having a session in which you are never ahead, and in doing so lose your capital. If you have $10,000, however, and frequently bet on the banker, your chances of trouncing every casino on The Strip are still very good indeed. Of course, you are not going to make any real money with this strategy, but you will be able to claim truthfully to have done something the greatest gamblers in the world have not done. Perhaps you will make a fortune when you sell your story to Hollywood.

Caveat Emptor

There are currently progression systems offered for sale through the Internet. Many are glossily advertised and come with the slick confident assurances of professional con men. All such systems are variants of existing progression systems. It is unreasonable to buy such systems because:

1. They don't work.
2. All progression systems operate on the same basic principles and are all, therefore, known.
3. They don't work.

Unfortunately, there is always a ready market of people who wish to make their fortunes quickly and painlessly. My way to riches is complex and requires study, but it does work. The ways of the system sellers are short and painless but lead nowhere.

There are a number of key phrases that mark out the system seller. Inevitably, their advertisement will have the word "free" in there somewhere, which is only playing with words, since there is always money to pay further down the line or they wouldn't be in business. They will often talk about baccarat in a pseudo-scientific manner, using words and phrases which may not be familiar to you but do sound impressive. They may talk about "real-world conditions." This is because any baccarat system currently available doesn't work, and, therefore, the result of any computer simulation would show this to be the case. So they will pretend that baccarat computer simulations are not mathematically the same as baccarat played in a casino. Of course, computer simulations are not as exciting as playing in the real casino, but that is another matter.

Most people never play enough baccarat in a lifetime to determine with absolute certainty that a system does or does not work. This is what the system seller knows. Note that game analysts typically require the results not of hundreds of hands, or millions of hands, but at the very least *tens* of millions of hands. Over one trillion hands were played to calculate the figures in this book. Most of the betting methods commercially available involve raising your bet after a series of losses. This means that the system buyer may well win more sessions than he loses, but he will win quite small amounts in his winning sessions and lose very large amounts in his losing sessions. If he is reasonably well financed, the system buyer will, initially, probably grind ahead with a series of wins.

Some of the people who use the system-seller's method will lose, curse their gullibility, and try to forget they were ever duped. Many will win, though, because baccarat is a game with such a small house take, where a lucky player could remain ahead of the game for some time, easily for a few thousand hands. The use of a system will not change the odds of the game in the slightest way, though the player naturally believes he has found the elixir of wealth and tells everyone about his wonderful secret, providing free publicity for the system seller. The player will defend his system to the death, even when it inevitably begins to lose. He can't give up now, he has invested himself emotionally in the system's success, and to admit defeat would mean accepting a crushing psychological blow. Because of the pattern of his losses, which will be infrequent and large, he will convince himself that it is merely a run of bad luck that is causing him to lose.

There is a new category of baccarat system seller emerging who pretends to sell winning card-counting systems. This is ingenious. After all, many people know that blackjack card-counters are barred from casinos, as this has been popularized in films such as *Rain Man*, so why would the same methods not work as well in baccarat? Well, as I will explain in Chapter 3, my reason for believing so is because the most brilliant minds in gambling have proved it cannot be done. There may be a very advanced card-counting strategy which could allow you to win to some extent, as I will explain, but if it does exist it would require extraordinary patience, dedication, and financial resources to be successful. The system sellers do not possess such a method, of that I am certain. They would have no incentive in doing so in any case, since it has been proven time and time again that advertising an easy strategy which does not work will be always be more commercially successful than trying to sell a difficult strategy which does.

I will not even mention that class of system seller who peddles astrology, fortune charms, or black magic to guarantee success at the table, fun as it may be. Well, okay, maybe I will. The issue is a little more relevant now because of the interest engendered by paranormal phenomena with a veneer of scientific respectability, such as extrasensory perception. If you had the ability to predict which cards would turn up a few seconds before they actually did, then baccarat would be a piece of cake. You could go into any casino with $20 and come out with $200 million. Unfortunately, there's no hard proof to suggest that ESP works. There is, however, a very real reason to believe in the even more unlikely force which causes people to believe a completely illogical and ridiculous explanation of something in preference to an ordinary and rational one. Perhaps there's an elite group of psychics turning the baccarat tables on Las Vegas as we speak—or perhaps not.

Many people will tell you that anyone who knew how to make money from gambling would use the system himself rather than sell it. In fact, this is only a half truth. There are systems which have been proven to make money at various forms of gambling, but they often require as much effort as you would put into any other career, and your earnings will be both variable and probably less than spectacular. The system sellers will tell you, however, that you can make a fortune both quickly and without any effort, but if there really were such an easy way to beat the house, then the casino industry would go broke in next to no time.

Does Mini-Baccarat Differ From Big-Table Baccarat?

Many players maintain that the odds in mini-baccarat are different from those in the main game. On the face of it, there would seem to be a possible basis for this claim. It is true that since the rules are identical there should be no difference between the odds of the two games; on the other hand, it may be that the different shuffling styles could cause different results.

A plausible scenario might be that cards sloppily shuffled from "new-deck" order would favor the player, the bank, or tie. New decks are ordered in the following sequences: Ace to King, Ace to King, King to Ace, King to Ace. Ten-valued cards will clump together, creating many zero-valued hands. It can be seen that cards dealt out in new-deck order will heavily favor the tie bet if no shuffling took place but of course this would never happen. Perhaps this tie bias could survive a simple shuffle?

I tested this idea on Dennis Suggs's "Baccarat Buster" software, which has the ability to simulate real-world shuffles. Unfortunately, with anything approaching the complexity of even the simplest casino shuffle, any inherent bias is removed and the various bets even out. For those of you who distrust computers and doubt their ability to simulate the myriad factors inherent in a real shuffle, there is data on actual games from Erick St. Germain in his *Seventy-two Days at the Baccarat Table*. The author analyzed thousands of shoes of both big-table baccarat and mini-baccarat. His conclusion: "If there is a difference, it is very tiny."

Of course, this depends very much on the shuffling practices of the casinos where St. Germain spent time studying, but in the absence of any contrary data, my suggestion is that the two versions of the game do not differ significantly, and my research has been conducted with this in mind.

This does not mean, however, that the respective shuffling processes are completely random, merely that a player with no knowledge of the ordering of the cards should assume that the expectations of the various bets are their ordinary mathematical ones.

Does Which Seat You Sit in Matter in Baccarat?

In other card games, such as blackjack and poker, seating position has an important effect on the odds and the correct playing strategy. This leads some people to believe that the same is true of baccarat. Because the game is purely mechanical with no scope for playing decisions, this is not, in fact, the case. Seating position only affects the ceremony of the game. In the older versions of baccarat, seating position is of some importance. In chemin de fer, seating position determines who will hold the bank most frequently, while in *baccarat en banque*, the active player on the second half of the table has useful information about the first player.

Women at the Baccarat Tables

The use of "he" in this book is primarily for convenience of language, though it also reflects the reality of the situation. Comparatively few women play in the baccarat pit (if they are not house employees). This is hardly surprising in the light of the fact that the gambling world is one of the last unreconstructed bastions of male chauvinism. The last forty years have apparently passed many casinos by, not to mention many gamblers.

The seemingly universal assumption among gamblers, and I'm talking about professional gamblers with Ph.D.s in mathematics as much as average Joe Hick, is that women know zip about gambling, and this seems unlikely to change dramatically in the near future. This is a self-fulfilling assumption, since few women are willing to brave the pungent stench of testosterone in order to become sufficiently knowledgeable about baccarat or other casino games.

Nevertheless, this situation benefits nobody; not the casinos, who are wasting a very profitable resource of consumers; not women in general, who doubtless would appreciate the escapist fantasy baccarat offers as much as the man next to them; and certainly not average Joe Hick, who sorely needs to spend more time in the company of women. My advice to the casinos is that they seriously consider how their staff behave towards women, which should be chivalrously and courteously without being patronizing—not because of some liberal politically-correct agenda, but because to do otherwise is to lose money.

Baccarat, with its understated aura and elegant procedures, would doubtless be a good starting point to bring women into gambling. There is something akin to the feminine mystique in the ritual of the game which a wise pit boss would do well to take advantage of.

3

Card-Counting

The techniques described in the next few chapters fall under the heading of "advantage play." This is a catch-all term used to describe any technique which is both legal and gives the player an advantage over the house. Prior to the publication of this book, it was widely assumed that no method existed which could give the player the ability to take on the casinos at baccarat. Many gambling books will tell you that there is no way to win consistently at baccarat. In fact, there are ways, though baccarat is by no means the easiest game at which to make money.

The first scientifically based approach to baccarat was that of card-counting. What follows is a concise history of the subject. Readers familiar with this subject may skip or skim through this section, which is intended to explain the concepts involved to a beginner.

Card-counting is an advanced gambling tool, which could in theory give a player the advantage in almost any card game. Card-counting was developed in the 1950s by Dr. Edward Thorp. Professor Thorp is so extraordinary that had he not really lived, as a character of fiction his exploits would have been dismissed as far-fetched. Unquestionably the greatest mind ever to turn his attention to gambling, Thorp has made small fortunes at blackjack, roulette, and sports betting; he also pioneered the incredibly successful "warrant-hedging" technique on the greatest gambling game of all, the stock market. Over $65 billion have passed through his hands over the last few decades, and his personal fortune can only be guessed at. He is without doubt the most successful gambler who has ever lived. All of this was due to an extraordinary ability to understand the mathematics of gambling games and devise practical systems to bend chance to his will.

Experimenting with the game of blackjack, Thorp discovered that when you remove certain cards from the deck, this alters the house advantage. He also found that a player could sometimes have the advantage over the house. For example, removing all the 5s from a deck puts the odds in the player's favor. These favorable situations are outnumbered by unfavorable ones, and so, on average, an unskilled player would lose more than he wins. Thorp discovered, however, if the player knows when he has the advantage, he can bet more than when the house has the advantage, and so win more money than he loses.

Thorp constructed his highly successful ten-count system, with which he won many thousands of dollars from the casinos at blackjack. They retaliated with a series of countermeasures designed to thwart the "counters," the disciples who read Thorp's bestselling *Beat the Dealer* and tried their own luck with his system. There are still some professional counters around today, although the casinos are wise to the danger and bar any player they suspect is counting.

How does counting work? Well, the most popular systems are called "point counts." Cards are given a value according to how good or bad their removal is for the player. Cards whose removal from the deck is bad are given a minus value, good cards are given a plus value. At all times, the counter keeps a running count in his head which begins at zero. Every time he sees a card he adds or subtracts its value from the running count in his head. When the running count is high (lots of plus cards are dealt) the player has the advantage and should bet more. When it is negative he should bet the minimum or leave the table. The ratio between the player's "large" and "small" bets is called his bet spread, and the larger it is, the more he will win. A typical count looks like this (this is the popular high-low count):

Ace	Ten	Nine	Eight	Seven	Six	Five	Four	Three	Two
−1	−1	0	0	0	+1	+1	+1	+1	+1

It is hard to guess at the amount of money casinos have lost to blackjack card-counters, but the figure is unlikely to be less than tens of millions of dollars. Thorp had discovered that rare thing, a gambling system which actually worked.

So, of what interest is this to baccarat players? Well, it is a little-known fact that card-counting can also be applied to baccarat. Thorp and other gambling mathematicians began searching around for other games to win at, and baccarat seemed the obvious choice. As in blackjack, the cards are dealt until the pack is depleted, then the cards are shuffled. Therefore, the odds of the various bets change, as one hand after another is dealt from the shoe.

Thorp and a fellow academic, William Walden, investigated the possibility of applying card-counting techniques to baccarat, and their work was recorded for posterity—at the taxpayer's expense—in "A Winning Bet in Nevada Baccarat" (*Journal of the American Statistical Association*, vol. 73, 1966). The work was an outgrowth of Walden's Ph.D. thesis, which Thorp supervised.

With the aid of a computer, Thorp and Walden determined the precise expectations for various bets. Then they analyzed random subsets of thirteen cards, a typical minimum number of cards remaining in a deck before a shuffle, to see if either the player or banker bet was favorable (the tie bet had not yet been introduced). In only two occasions out of fifty-eight did Thorp and Walden discover any advantage. Once the player had an edge of 3.2 percent; once the banker had an edge of 0.1 percent. Clearly, they concluded, no system based on card-counting could yield a practical winning strategy, for the favorable situations were just too infrequent.

There were two main reasons why the application of card-counting techniques would not work in baccarat, though they had been proven so successful in blackjack. First, the game is dealt from eight or six decks, whereas blackjack was originally dealt from only one. Thus, the original order of the cards is slower to change with multiple decks. Second, the approximate 1 percent disadvantage the bettor faces on the player and banker bets, while small when compared with most other casino games, is quite large when compared with blackjack, which is typically 0.5 percent or less (assuming skilled play).

The Effects of Removing a Single Card
From an Eight-Deck Baccarat Shoe

Card	Change in Advantage of Player Bet	Change in Advantage of Banker Bet
0	−0.002%	+0.002%
I	−0.004%	+0.004%
2	−0.005%	+0.005%
3	−0.007%	+0.007%
4	−0.012%	+0.012%
5	+0.008%	−0.008%
6	+0.011%	−0.011%
7	+0.008%	−0.008%
8	+0.005%	−0.005%
9	+0.003%	−0.003%

In a footnote to the text, however, Thorp stated that a strategy might be feasible when technology progressed further, and that, in any case, he only ruled out strategies based on card-counting. He added, intriguingly, that strategies based on an analysis of card-shuffling might produce a winning method.

At that time, casinos also offered two side bets in addition to the main part of the game, depending on whether or not the bankers' first two cards would total 8 or 9, which paid off at 9 to 1. Under ordinary circumstances, these bets had a large house advantage of approximately 5 percent, but the academics discovered that when there was a large number of 8s or 9s remaining to be dealt, i.e., less than the average number of 9s and 8s had been dealt, these bets became advantageous to the player. They designed a card-counting system to exploit these favorable opportunities. Because these situations were not too frequent, occurring only 10 percent of the time in every shoe, it was necessary for a winning system-player to raise his bets by a factor of forty in order to counter the attrition of the many small waiting bets he would have to make.

With a team of trained players, the two went to Nevada with a highly successful application of their system. Thorp records in his book *Beat the Dealer* that the team averaged $100 an hour in the first casino they visited. After five nights, Thorp was under scrutiny. After the seventh night the team was barred. In the next casino they visited they raised their stakes. They averaged $1,000 an hour for two hours before they were barred again. Then the side bets disappeared, throughout the state, never to return. Perhaps this was for the best, for in a Las Vegas which still had close connections with the mob, it is unlikely that the team would have been allowed to go on winning indefinitely.

It seems somewhat surprising that no other card players had discovered for themselves the system which Thorp and his associates used, particularly since the system was so simple, and the importance of card removal in blackjack and the European forms of baccarat was already recognized (though not fully understood). Perhaps they were more adept at concealing their methods.

Shortly afterward, a side bet began to appear on the tables which paid 8 or 9 to one whenever the result of a hand was tied. This gradually became a standard feature of the game.

Interest in the application of mathematics to baccarat remained largely dormant for the next decade.

David Sklansky, one of the more innovative of gambling writers, discovered that if the last six cards dealt from a baccarat shoe were three 2s and three 3s, the player bet enjoyed an 80 percent advantage. The banker bet enjoys a similar advantage if only 7s and 8s remain in the deck. Sklansky stated that card-counting may indeed be possible at baccarat, and suggested devising a count which weighed 2s and 3s against 7s and 8s.

In March 1982, the *Gambling Times* published a series of six-card subsets which could give the player an advantage at the very end of the deck. This inspired Joel Friedman to investigate all possible six-card subsets. He discovered that a player with computer-perfect knowledge of the last six-card subsets could gain an average profit of 26 percent on that hand. By raising his bets fourfold (or more), his profits could outweigh the loss from making the approximately eighty "waiting" bets on the banker that the player would have to make in order to earn the right to bet on this last hand. More than 24 percent of his gain would come from the tie bet. This finding seemed strange, considering the tie bet is almost always disregarded by expert opinion as a frivolous wager that only a fool would make, since it is fourteen times less favorable than the bank or player bets. As Friedman's study showed, however, the tie advantage changes much more rapidly than the player or the banker. The tie is like a golden chalice in a snake pit.

It was left to Peter Griffin, the world's leading authority on the mathematics of blackjack, to investigate the matter fully in his *Theory of Blackjack*. After producing a rendition of the history of the subject of card-counting in baccarat, Griffin presented his "ultimate point count," so called because it would be impossible to design a more powerful count for the game. The count values are given below:

Card	Player Bet	Bank Bet	Tie
Ace	−1.86	1.82	5.37
2	−2.25	2.17	−9.93
3	−2.79	2.69	−8.88
4	−4.96	4.80	−12.13
5	3.49	−3.43	−10.97
6	4.69	−4.70	−48.12
7	3.39	−3.44	−45.29
8	2.21	−2.08	27.15
9	1.04	−0.96	17.68
10	0.74	−0.78	21.28
House Edge	−1.235%	−1.057	−14.359

Why does the removal of certain cards favor certain bets, while some cards make other bets less favorable? Well, you can see from Griffin's table that the tie bet becomes more attractive if a lot of 6s are unplayed. This is explained by the fact that should either the first or second player cards be a 6, then they are more likely to be paired with a zero-valued card than any other, giving a total of 6. If the bank hand is also a 6, then the hand is a tie and no further cards are drawn. If the bank hand counts less than 6, then another card will be drawn, effectively giving the bank another chance to equal the player's total (from the tie bettor's perspective). Only a bank total of 7, 8, or 9 results in an automatic loss for the tie bet. In this instance, the tie is heavily favored. Such a situation is more frequent if there are many 6s waiting to be dealt.

The explanation for the changes in advantage with the player and bank bets is a little more complex. Basically, the discrepancy is caused by the difference between the player's fairly crude rules for drawing a third card and the bank's comparatively sophisticated decisions based on the turn of the player's card. Griffin's count weighs cards of value from 1 to 4 against those from 5 to 9 (10-valued cards make little difference either way). It can be seen that this relates directly to the instructions for the player with a total from 0 to 5 for drawing a third card.

A high number of cards of value from Ace through to 4 increases the chances of the player bettering his total, while a high number of cards valued 4 through 9 increases the likelihood that the player hand will worsen, and more often than not the bank will stand in this situation. Note that the bank hand will tend to stand on winning totals more often than the player hand.

The bank hand is comparatively unaffected by these phenomena, as its more intelligent rules mean that certain cards benefit or hinder the bank, depending on the composition of the hand dealt. Nonetheless, it gains or loses according to the player's increased or decreased likelihood of drawing to a good total. It also helps the bank to have a surplus of high cards when it has a total against which it must draw, i.e., 0, 1, or 2, as these cards are likely to benefit the hand more than a low total.

Griffin explains how his count works:

Suppose the first hand out of the shoe uses a 3 and a 4 for the player and a 9 and a Jack for the bank. Our running count (for the bank bet) is $2.69 + 4.80 - 0.96 + 0.78 = 7.31$. Now don't plunge into the bank bet just because we have a positive count! Rather, divide it by the number of remaining cards, which is $416 - 4 = 412$. You estimate the bank expectation to be:

$-1.059 + 7.31/412 = -1.04016$.

So the shoe is not quite ready for us.

Clearly, Griffin was not intending this for practical use. It would be impossible to make such complicated calculations in the short time available between hands, even with the aid of a scorecard. Griffin was trying to create the most powerful count he could, and if that could not beat the game, then a less powerful, more usable count could not do any better. After running many computer simulations, Griffin concluded that if a player bet $1,000 every time his count indicated an advantage and did not bet otherwise, he would make three bets a day and would earn, on average, 7 cents a day. This is only if all the cards are dealt out, something which no casino would ever do. The problem is that unlike in blackjack, where the advantage between player and dealer can change wildly, the removal of a card in baccarat has very little effect on the odds of the game.

The problem is that while Friedman's analysis was correct, cards are never dealt right to the end in the real world; typically, ten to twenty cards are removed, or burned (placed face down at the start of the deal). If the value of even a few cards is kept from the player's knowledge, his earning potential is dramatically reduced. For example, with ten cards remaining, a player with computer-perfect information has an earning potential of 3 percent of whatever he bets on this hand, nine times less than with six cards remaining, and in the real world, it is unusual for the cards to be dealt this deeply.

Also, Griffin's tie count actually lost money, even though it was only supposed to be wagering on favorable situations. There are a number of reasons for this. First, Griffin recognized and produced data to confirm that as the pack was depleted, the accuracy of his count system diminished. At the very end of the deck it was very unreliable indeed, precisely when any favorable situations, infrequent as they were, would occur. Second, Griffin assumed that the average probability of a tie remained constant, at 14.35 percent. In fact, this is not the case. As more of the pack is dealt, the tie becomes less favorable. This is known as the "floating advantage." To illustrate, if you play baccarat from a single deck, the tie has an expectation of 15.7 percent. When card-counting, all of the favorable situations we can raise our wager on—according to Griffin's count system—occur with only half to a quarter deck or less remaining, so the tie expectation is even worse. Consequently, our count system will be telling us to make many bets when we have no advantage.

Griffin provides us with a table which seems to prove this hypothesis. He gives us data about the actual expectation of the various bets when thirteen cards are remaining, and their estimated expectation according to his count system. Sure enough, the tie count's estimate is significantly higher than its actual expectation. Moreover, Griffin's bank count underestimates its actual advantage, while the player count overestimates its actual advantage, while the player count overestimates it. This is in accordance with the "floating edge" hypothesis, as the bank bet becomes more favorable with fewer decks, at the expense of the player. For more information on this very complicated subject, see Appendix C.

Thorp backed up Griffin's findings in *The Mathematics of Gambling* (1981), stating that the removal of a card in baccarat was nine times less bearing on the results than in blackjack. Few were prepared to attack these widely respected authors' findings, but one source of dissent came from the 1992 book *The Money-Spinners*, by Englishman "Jacques Black" (as a blackjack card-counter, his identity needed to be kept secret from the casinos). Black had used a simplified derivation of Griffin's count system for the bank and player in several London casinos, and made a profit of 2,000 English pounds. However, he himself was unsure whether this was not merely a chance fluctuation from an expected negative result that would reveal itself in time.

Black's work sparked my initial interest in baccarat. He describes how casinos have a lethal arsenal of techniques to prevent card-counting in blackjack, but none to prevent counting in baccarat. This, he admitted, was largely because the most brilliant gambling mathematicians believed it could not be done. If a count could be devised to win at baccarat, a player could bet any sum he chose and become wealthy beyond his dreams. He could play whenever he chose, renounce his life as a hired hand, and become a professional gambler, beholden to no one. Moreover, as with Edward Thorp, he would become a famous and respected figure.

Black's contention was that Griffin used a pessimistic model with which to calculate his results. Griffin assumed an eight-deck American baccarat shoe took over an hour to deal. Black's experience playing six-deck London Punto Banco was that it took only thirty to forty minutes to deal out a shoe. Since more hands played per hour meant a greater number of favorable opportunities on which to bet, the player's earnings could be increased by seeking out faster games, such as Black describes. (In fact, some mini-baccarat dealers can get through six decks in ten minutes.)

Black also recognized that the higher table maximums available in baccarat made it possible to see a large absolute return in terms of money won even if the advantage gained was very small. Finally, he noted that the cut-card was extremely deep in the deck, remarking that in the first game he played the cut-card was located eight cards from the bottom. Griffin assumed that before the final hand was dealt, the minimum number of cards remaining, in even the best games, was no fewer than ten. This difference is very significant.

I created a computer program to simulate a game of baccarat to see for myself whether Black's count works. Unfortunately, it does not. Black's reasoning is fundamentally flawed. I concluded that the banker and player bets are too symmetrical for the purposes of card-counting; neither bet is significantly favored by the removal of a particular card. Considering, for example, that any hand comprised of four cards has perfect symmetry, the composition of the deck has no effect at all on such a hand, since what is good for the player is good for the banker. So one-third of all hands are completely unaffected by card removal. The slight discrepancies which occur between player and banker with five- or six-card hands are just that—slight.

Then I tested further count systems, some of my own creation, some created by others. All exhibited a loss or an expectation too small to be of any practical value. I finally tried Griffin's "ultimate point count," and found that his results were confirmed by my own.

End-Play—The Silicon Method

I wondered if a computer might play with enough accuracy to allow me to play baccarat with a worthwhile advantage. Computers to play blackjack and to predict the path of a roulette ball have been both designed and successfully tested in the casino. Their operators concealed the devices in their shoes and decoded the information they received through a series of electric vibrations. There are places in the world where use of a computer is not necessarily illegal. Nevada isn't one of them, and use of a computer there may lead to a jail sentence. Atlantic City doesn't allow it either, although there the maximum punishment you can get is comparatively small considering the potential rewards. Some European countries have no specific legislation to prevent the use of a computer.

A computer could tell me exactly when any of the three bets was favorable. All I had to do was tell it which cards had been dealt. Unfortunately, when I wrote a program to detect advantageous situations on my home computer the results were not spectacular. With a game dealt down to ten cards and perfect wagering any time there was a favorable situation, I could expect to earn approximately 4.5 percent per shoe on whatever amount I bet. (There are some games in which you may get a cut-card only nine or eight cards deep, seven if you can see the bottom card, so you may be able to earn much more than this.)

So, if I bet $1,000 every time my computer told me I had an edge, I'd make $45 for every shoe I played. I'd also have to make some unfavorable bets earlier in the shoe, since I couldn't just sit at the table doing nothing, and this would dilute my advantage further. If I played two shoes in an hour I'd make at most $110 an hour, or $880 in a working day. With a little trickery (for example, by betting only on the banker after a series of player wins, a typical strategy) I would be losing roughly $14 a hour, or $112 a day on my unfavorable wagers, leaving $768. This is still a very good wage, but it's quite a small return on investment—and I didn't have the money to bet at such high levels anyway, without an unacceptable risk of ruin. If I did, I would have kept on doing what made me the money in the first place.

The costs of devising a concealed computer are themselves

prohibitive, and the project would be unrewarding compared to devising a computer to assist you at other forms of gambling. For example, computers devised to predict the path of a roulette ball can give you a 44 percent edge on *every wager.* (A better approach to winning at baccarat via computer would be to design one to analyze simple shuffles. It's theoretically possible to track a shuffle with a hidden camera and feed the data into a computer. You could then predict the value of every card with a high degree of certainty as they are dealt. Simpler devices have already been tested to analyze successive card shuffles with a spectacular degree of success.)

My research wasn't entirely wasted, though. I estimated that 80 or 90 percent of the earnings a computer could make from baccarat could be won by a human of reasonable intelligence. This is because most of the profit comes from recognizing when the tie bet is *extremely* favorable, i.e. over 50 percent. The contribution of the occasional favorable bank and player bets is unimportant. So are the relatively small advantages which occur for the tie bet, and determining when the tie bet is very favorable is not impossible.

There was one acknowledged gambling authority whose methodology appeared sound and who believed in the potential of a winning baccarat system. Mike Caro, a gambling pioneer known chiefly for his work on the application of body language to poker, wrote in *Caro on Gambling* (1984) that he had run 120 computer simulations of 2,500 sample baccarat hands. He detected 7 situations out of 120 when ties yielded a profit of 15 percent or more. This led Caro to speculate that a counting system based on combinations of cards for the tie wager might be successful. Note that it's not difficult to find games with more cards dealt out.

Caro argues that there are a number of generalizations that can be made. The gambler has an advantage on the tie bet

If 75 percent of the remaining cards are 10s, 6s, and 7s.
If 70 percent of the deck contains 5s, 4s, 3s, 2s, and Aces.
If 50 percent of the deck is composed of 6s and 7s.

Caro's simulations were based on an analysis of twenty card subsets. His conclusions were tentative, and he made no pretense of the fact that further work would be required to determine the viability of his ideas with statistical confidence. Note, however, how Caro's simulation results differ from Griffin's. This can be attributed to the greater sample size of Griffin's study, but also indicates how difficult it is to restrict the variance of the volatile tie bet.

The "Perfect" Bet

Another simple idea, which I'm sure many players must have considered, is expressed in Roger Gros's *How to Win at Casino Gambling* (1993). It was the suggestion of an anonymous baccarat supervisor in Atlantic City in the late 1970s. Gros elaborates:

> Since face cards and 10s are worth nothing in baccarat, this supervisor suggested that if you could count all the cards that are dealt in baccarat and determine that all the cards remaining when the yellow card appears are 10s or face cards, you know a nothing-nothing tie will be declared on the last hand. A player with that knowledge could then place the maximum bet on the tie...The problem is that the odds on the final ten or fifteen cards being all 10s or face cards are pretty high.

Very high, in fact. With eight cards remaining, the most optimistic level of penetration you are likely to receive, the chance of only 10s and face cards remaining, is less than .007 of 1 percent. In a real game, of course, the number of cards cut out of play, or burned, will typically be more than this. This makes this improbable event a negligible second-order possibility. With sixteen cards remaining, for example, the event will occur every few hundred million times, or every couple of ice ages. Moreover, Gros doesn't explain how you might actually go about determining when this wildly unlikely situation might arise. This is fairly simple, though; there are 288 non–ten-valued cards in the deck. Note down a notch on your scorecard every time you see a card other than ten, and when you reach 288, only 10s remain.

Nonetheless, the idea got me thinking. Plainly, it was unnecessary for the deck to be so extreme (rich with tens). If the deck was composed mostly of 10s, the player might still have a large advantage. Then it occurred to me that a successful counting system would detect concentrations of cards, which were not intrinsically good or bad for the tie, in small subsets. Therefore, a point-count system would be of no use; the player would have to achieve close to computer-perfect play. This can be done by striking off the cards as they are dealt on the casino tally sheet, or scorecard. Then the player can know the exact composition of the cards remaining to be dealt, and analyze the composition for favorable tie wagers. If the tie bet is favorable, he can put down a very large wager, since the odds are in his favor. Of course, this may attract attention and suspicion from casino personnel, particularly if the player is winning, so it may be advisable to develop some form of coded notation for this purpose.

With compositions composed of a quarter deck or less, 10s become very important in determining favorable tie wagers. Note that this result is contrary to Griffin's findings. This is because late in the deck, the increased fluctuation means the number of 10s tends to dominate the deck structure. The following table explains how extreme numbers of 10s can give the player an edge:

Cards Remaining	Tens Necessary for Tie Advantage	+ One Pair
6	6	4
7	6	6
8	6	5
9	7	6
10	8	6
11	8	7
12	9	8
13	10	9
14	10	
15	11	
16	11	
17	12	
18	12	
19	13	
20	14	

Regardless of other considerations, with less than thirteen cards, a player should avoid the tie, if three or more single cards of a positive value (other than a 10 or a face-card) are present. So, for example, eight 10s, one Ace, one 2, one 7, or one 9 is an unfavorable tie wager. Single cards are helpful to the tie bet only when there are two whose combined value is 10, e.g., one 6 remains and one 4 remains, and there are a disproportionate number of 10s remaining.

I have found Caro's suggestions a useful guideline. In addition, a player should always assume a tie advantage if:

1. All the cards in the deck are even.
2. There are no more than three cards of a particular value remaining in the deck, e.g., only 3s, 5s, and 10s remain to be dealt.
3. There are two 7s remaining with less than ten cards left.
4. There are two 7s and two 6s with less than twelve cards left.

There are other peculiar deck subsets which exhibit a positive expectation for the tie for no apparent reason. For example, when every card value has precisely two cards remaining (i.e., two 10s, two 9s, two 8s, etc.), the tie has a slight edge. To track all the myriad situations is clearly not possible, but by following these recommendations you may be able to capture the lion's share of expected value.

The full strategy for determining favorable tie situations is beyond the scope of this book. Nevertheless, you have the most vital elements of the strategy already.

The advantage distribution for the tie is comparatively stable when the deck structure is intact, hence the small effects of removal calculated by Griffin. Conventional linear count systems, however, assume a standard deck, and with extreme concentrations of cards in small subsets this assumption can be wildly inaccurate. The huge shifts in edge which are necessary to detect in order to gain an advantage, occur with the rise in the total number of denominations eliminated from the pack, although the specific denominations are relatively unimportant. To a certain extent, this is empirically verifiable. With only one card of any value remaining, the tie wager enjoys an advantage of between 500 and 800 percent. With two denominations, the advantage falls slightly, as the possible number of outcomes is doubled.

By the time we reach five or six denominations, the advantage (if any) becomes marginal. This "concentration theory" is not only relevant to baccarat, it is a necessary addition to the fundamental theory of card-counting, and to the mathematics of sampling without replacement.

To learn these rules, and to note the cards accurately as they are dealt, may seem daunting. Actually, with application the task becomes relatively easy and can be learned perfectly with a few months practice.

When a player does detect a favorable situation, he will never know his precise advantage, a serious drawback to this system because it can lead to overbetting. It should not, however, unduly trouble the well-financed player. When these occur, the advantages are often high—on average around 20 percent—though they can rise to as much as 450 percent. I once detected a situation in which there were only 10s and 5s in the deck, which yielded approximately that great of an edge. A bet of $10,000 resulted in a win of $90,000!

Ideally, while waiting for the end of the shoe, a player should wager only on the bank hand, possibly betting only every other hand so as to appear to be following some trending system and saving money, and betting the minimum. When you get to the last hand, try betting a peculiar amount (though preferably small) on the bank, which will slow down the game enough to give you time to analyze the remaining cards for an advantage. I typically raise my bets by fifty times the table minimum, which, surprisingly, has never drawn me any heat. Other players I have known spread from $5 to $10,000 on a regular basis. Such a strategy, however, requires a large bankroll.

The chief drawback to this system is that you need the patience of a saint, as favorable end-deck compositions occur very, very rarely. This is a very big drawback. You will find a favorable tie wager perhaps one shoe in thirty, though this varies greatly with the number of exposed cards. For the vast majority of gamblers, this is an unacceptably long time to wait for a good bet. When they do occur, however, they are the most favorable opportunities you will find in any form of gambling.

There are certain tricks to make this system more attractive. In games with European-style penetration, where no cards are cut out of play, you will occasionally come across dealers who accidentally expose the burn cards. In some cases, you will be able to know the values of all the cards dealt, making your edge substantially higher, frequently exceeding 100 percent, particularly if the deck is dealt down to the last card. Remember, your earning potential is an average 24 percent of your bet if you have perfect knowledge of the last six cards. Much of this gain will come from situations in which you have four 10s and a pair, or four 10s and two other cards whose value adds up to 10.

To find such clumsy dealers is not easy. To make money consistently you will need a team to scout for such opportunities. I have found that female dealers with small hands are most likely to make this error. You will usually only be able to see the cards at a certain angle, so your seating position will be crucial. This will vary from dealer to dealer.

Alternatively, you can place an agent, or "spook," directly behind the dealer, who can then signal to you the value of the burn cards dealt. This practice is currently a legal grey area in Nevada, though it may not be elsewhere. Depending on the number of cards you can "spook," you will be able to spread your bet less dramatically than would normally be the case. If you can see all the burn cards, a 1 to 10 bet spread will be sufficient to generate attractive profits.

Another method is to abandon any game in which an excess number of 10s have been dealt. This method is known as back-counting, or "Wonging" (after the master gambler Stanford Wong, who first popularized this technique at the blackjack tables). Tens play a crucial role in the very large advantages it is possible to get on the last hand. If a lot of 10s have already been dealt, your chance of getting a favorable wager on the tie is very small, and you are probably wasting your time continuing to play through the shoe. My recommendation would be to abandon any game where the ratio of 10s to other cards falls below .30, more or less the initial ratio of 10s to other cards in the deck. This will significantly boost your expected value per shoe by almost double the figures given by Griffin. It does mean, however, abandoning games, probably more than might be considered practical.

It may be possible to determine a better method of knowing when to leave the game, for example, by determining that the number of cards remaining for each denomination at each stage of the deck are not

sufficiently different from their expected values to suggest the
possibility of a favorable tie wager at the conclusion of the shoe. But this
is a task for future generations.

In summary, it is certainly possible to make money at baccarat by
card-counting if you are prepared to undertake a great deal of study, are
adequately financed, possessed of great powers of concentration, and
able to bet from the table minimum to the table maximum without
attracting attention—but you might well be better off using those
qualities to make a fortune elsewhere.

For the expert player in the most favorable games, it certainly would
be possible to break even, or maybe make small profits. He could then
enjoy free casino complimentaries for the rest of his days. Even to break
even, however, requires at least a spread of 1 to 30 (in a six-deck game,
assuming every hand is played). This requires a huge bankroll.
Moreover, the slightest mistake will obliterate your advantage. Also,
there is no easy way to hide an increase in your bets by a factor of thirty
on the last hand. This will undoubtedly cause suspicion on the part of
the casino—and favorable bets are very, very rare.

A Simple Social Count to Lose Less

For the player who does not wish to go to the great lengths necessary to
win at baccarat, but who simply wants the pride of playing better than
nearly all of his fellow gamblers, to play for comps (see Chapter 12), or
to follow a system other than the hypnotically stupid trending systems
described elsewhere, then I present you with a simple card-counting
system.

If you want to lose a little less and do not mind extending a little
effort, try the following scheme: use Thorp's count, not to determine
when to raise your bets, but to determine which hand to bet on in order
to minimize your losses. Because the player and bank hand have very
similar house advantages, often the (very slight) effects of removal will
cause the least advantageous bet—the one that makes least money for
the house—to intermittently switch between bank and player. How
much can you save from doing this? Well, on average, almost 8 percent
of your wager. You could look at this as a savings of $80 on every $1,000,

or one bet in every twelve, and it begins to look attractive. This amount may be slightly more or slightly less, depending on the amount of cards dealt. Here is the system:

Card	Point Value
Ace	1
2	1
3	2
4	2
5	−1
6	−2
7	−2
8	−1
9	0
10	0

How do we use this count? Starting at 0, add or subtract a total in your head or write it down on your scorecard. For example, write "player draws 7 (count −2, total −2) and 4 (count +2, total = 0), banker draws 3 and 4 (count +2, +2, total = 4). The total is called the running count. Divide this total by the number of decks remaining. There is no need to be too exact about this; you can do this by looking at the discard tray and estimating the number of cards that have been dealt. A simpler way is to count the number of hands. A hand of baccarat uses about five cards on average, so (almost) every time another hand is dealt, one-tenth of a deck is depleted. So, after every ten hands another deck is gone. Our final total, (running count) ÷ (number of decks remaining), is called the true count. Whenever you have a true count of −1 or less, bet on the player. Whenever you have a total of greater than −1, bet on the banker.

This system is not as accurate as Griffin's, but my experience in designing other card-counting systems for games such as *trente et quarante*, blackjack, and Red Dog, suggests that greatly simplifying the complexity of a very powerful system produces little measurable loss in performance, providing that the bet advantage is basically linear. The loss is unlikely to be more than 3 or 4 percent worse than Griffin's system. Actually, using all three counts suggested by Griffin would result in my count losing you less money, since Griffin's tie count would lose the money gained by his bank and player counts.

How can we improve on this system? Well, first of all, we can play with only six decks. Our card count will save us slightly more in the six-deck game because in the first two decks of an eight-deck shoe the advantage will change very slowly, and counting provides us only with a fractional gain over simply betting on the banker on every hand. In a six-deck game, you will save about 12 percent of your wager, or $120 per $1,000 bet, assuming you play every hand.

Most of your savings come later in the shoe, especially on the last deck. For this reason I would advise not betting at all, or betting the table minimum, until the second half of the shoe, although you must still count down the shoe while you are waiting. This can be a very effective strategy for maximizing your comp value. Try to look for a game where as many cards as possible are being dealt. Card-counting is more effective in a game where ten cards are cut out of play than thirty cards.

We could use a more complicated system, such as the two-parameter system suggested by Downton and Lockwood in Chapter 8. We could incorporate adjustments to the count for the floating advantage. We could attempt to devise a practical system for the tie bet. But this would involve a degree of difficulty which the recreational player would find off-putting.

The Secret Wager

For the player who's not interested in just minimizing losses, but wants to pull off a spectacular coup (perhaps using the maximum boldness strategy suggested in Chapter 2), knowing how to count cards will allow him to place a bet when the house advantage is nonexistent, or, provided he is patient, when he actually has the edge. Wait until the count has become very positive or very negative, above or below at least 20. The more extreme the count the higher your advantage. Such situations aren't all that common; this will probably only ever occur in the last few hands of a shoe. Depending on how fast the game is dealt, how many decks are used, and how many cards are dealt, you might have four to ten opportunities in an eight-hour day. In this situation, you will have a very slight advantage over the casino (somewhere between 0.1 and 0.5 percent). You can then place a wager of whatever size you want with the knowledge that chance is on your side. This is the only casino game in which you would be able to do this. Other games, such as roulette and craps, never give you an advantage. A blackjack player can detect situations in which he has the edge over the house, but to prevent detection he must not raise his bet too drastically, or he will be thrown out of the casino. This won't happen to you at baccarat, since very few people know how to count cards at this game.

Finally, in a game with a 4 percent commission (or less), counting cards is not worthwhile. In this situation, the player bet will only very rarely be more favorable than the banker.

4

Analyzing the Shuffle

So far the statistics given with regard to the player's expectation have been calculated on the basis that the shuffle is entirely random, that is, every card has an exactly equal chance of finishing in any position in the deck. In fact, this is a virtually impossible feat for even the most proficient croupier. Richard Epstein likened a random shuffle to a drunken inebriate scattering the cards in the air and retrieving them while blindfolded. At this point, Professor Edward Thorp reenters the story. In a little known paper in the *Journal of the Royal Statistical Society* entitled "Nonrandom Shuffling With Application to the Game of Faro," he wrote:

> Card games have been played for centuries, and today hundreds are well-known. There is an extensive literature of the heuristic, and to a lesser extent, of the mathematical analyses of these games. Virtually without exception, these treatments tacitly or explicitly assume random shuffling.... It is surprising, because the play of many games is altered by the nonrandomness of human shuffling. In particular, this nonrandomness yields simple winning strategies at blackjack, baccarat, and faro.

How can we tell whether a shuffle is random or not? Thorp goes on to describe how to do this. The simple method is described below:

1. Note down the order of the cards as they are dealt from an entire shoe.
2. Note the order of the cards as they are dealt in at least ten subsequent shoes.
3. Take this data away from the casino and analyze it.
4. Have a look at your data and see if anything strikes you as evidence of the process being nonrandom. It might be that, say, a pattern appears of blocks of cards being one or two apart, followed by a block of cards that are at large, random intervals.

In fact, the effects of nonrandom shuffling at baccarat were already well documented. This phenomenon predated the existence of the modern forms of baccarat dating back to the heyday of chemin de fer throughout France and in Monte Carlo. The casino operators observed that ordinary shuffling did not sufficiently break up the order of the cards. Consequently, entire hands would repeat from one shoe to the next. This knowledge could be exploited by perceptive players. Therefore, the casinos instituted complex procedures to break up the order of every distinct six-card sequence. These procedures survive to this day.

Richard Epstein's *Theory of Gambling and Statistical Logic* provided the first (and only) detailed analysis of card shuffling. Epstein conducted actual shuffles rather than computer-simulated ones and wrote, "It was found that highly expert shufflers create sequences in single-card interlacings approximately eight times as frequent as two-card interlacings: a group of three cards appears less than once per shuffle...It is evident from this operation that a large measure of orderliness is preserved for a small number of shuffles." The study recorded single-card interlacings 80 percent of the time, two cards 18 percent, and three cards 5 percent.

Anthony Curtis, editor of the *Las Vegas Advisor*, conducted a similar experiment. He obtained empirical data from four professional Las Vegas dealers who interleaved single cards 66 percent of the time, two cards 26 percent, three cards 5 percent, four cards 2 percent, and five cards less than 1 percent. While there are substantial differences between the two studies, it is evident that a player may, at least in theory, be able to predict cards to be dealt based on his knowledge of the shuffle and the previous deck order.

Currently, in the majority of casinos, very great pains are taken to try to randomize the deck. Often the cards are "washed" before shuffling. This involves taking three or more decks at a time, placing the cards face down on the felt, and moving them back and forth like in a washing machine for at least a minute. This breaks up the new-deck card sequences, which eliminates most of the deck order. A fine riffle shuffle can then be used to separate blocks of cards. Moreover, the discards are often not inserted into a discard tray, which would preserve their order, but into a big can which allows them to fall about in an unordered sequence. At big-table baccarat, new cards may well be brought in after every shoe.

The procedure at the smaller tables is very different. Often mini-baccarat dealers do not bother with these complex processes and use a blackjack-style discard tray. Sometimes a casino will simply slap a mini-baccarat felt on a blackjack table. The gaming industry is clearly unaware of the reasons for the elaborate shuffling of a baccarat shoe and treats it simply as a ceremonial measure.

With three riffles of six or eight decks, there is a slight correlation between the two-card sequences of a pack of cards dealt before a shuffle and after. This correlation is probably not exploitable. Sometimes you may find shuffles which are less thorough.

With the sloppiest of one-pass shuffles, it is possible you may be able to predict the order of entire hands as they repeat. In cases where the proper procedure is not followed, the game may be vulnerable to the method described next.

Sequential Shuffle-Tracking

A possible source of profit from baccarat is sequential shuffle-tracking, a highly advanced technique that has been passed down by word of mouth through an elite circle of blackjack players for the last two decades. It is also known as card-tracking, card location, key-carding, and the signature-card technique. It is based on the nonrandomness of human shuffling. It is an idea that is simple in concept, but not in practice.

In sloppy shuffles, much card order is preserved from one deck to the next. This means the cards are not broken up properly. Consequently, sequences of cards in the preshuffled deck may occur again in the postshuffled deck. This is particularly the case with eight decks of cards, which are very difficult to randomize by shuffling alone. Recent studies indicate that nine shuffles must be performed for eight decks to be fully randomized, although for baccarat this figure is deceptive, owing to the irrelevance of face cards and suits, which means fewer distinct cards to mix up.

A sequential tracker observes the cards not as they are dealt, but as they are put into the discard pile. He watches for sequences of cards that are unbroken by the shuffle, so that he can predict which card will appear next. If, for example, he sees the Ace of Clubs, followed by the Ace of Spades and the Jack of Hearts, removed in order in the preshuffled deck, and then sees the Ace of Clubs followed by the Ace of Spades in the postshuffled deck, he knows there is a good chance the Jack of Hearts is likely to follow.

The odds given for the game so far have been based on the assumption that the cards are dealt in a random fashion, or that the player has no knowledge of the nonrandomness of the deck, which is the same thing mathematically. If the player can exploit this knowledge, however, the odds can change.

What is done is simply this: in order to predict the occurrence of a card, watch a pack of cards dealt out. Say you wish to predict when the 9 of Spades will appear. When it appears, note the two cards preceding it, say, the Ace of Spades and the Jack of Hearts. If they go into the discard tray in the same sequence, then you're in business. After the shuffle, wait for these two "signature" cards to come out. If the Ace of Spades and the Jack of Hearts come out in the same order with only a few cards separating them, there is a good chance that the 9 of Spades is not far behind, perhaps in the next six cards. This phenomena happens because of the riffling style of trained dealers, and can only be eliminated by using a greater number of riffles. The casinos don't always do this, because more time spent shuffling means fewer hands are dealt, and the fewer hands that are dealt, the less money they make.

This method is very powerful indeed. It can be used in any card game where the shuffle is nonrandom. If a player can develop sequential tracking skills, he can master blackjack, poker, bridge, gin rummy, canasta, or any game he chooses. If this method were widely publicized, I have no doubt the casino industry would have serious trouble remaining financially viable. To apply it to baccarat, however, is another matter.

The problem is that knowing a certain card will appear within the next six cards doesn't give you an advantage on any of the three bets. This is because the card could end up in the bank or player hand. In our above example, knowing the 9 of Spades would appear as the first card would give us a large advantage on the player hand, but it might end up in the bank hand, so the advantage cancels out. In fact, we don't even know with 100 percent certainty that the card will appear within the next six cards, since even the worst of shuffles will give our prediction method only about 60 percent certainty. Card location, at least the way it is used in blackjack, is of no use in baccarat.

This would seem to suggest that this method is a dead end for the advantage player. I initially abandoned the idea as a nonstarter, but certain events came to my attention that led me to think otherwise. First, I obtained a copy of the *Griffin Mug Book*, a tome which lists advantage players and cheaters from around the world who prey on casinos, which is compiled yearly by the Griffin detective agency. There were about twenty snapshots, taken by casino surveillance, of individuals who were listed as "baccarat locators," accompanied by a brief description of what was undoubtedly a form of card location. Second, there were several high-profile wins by teams of players operating at baccarat, most notably at the Las Vegas Tropicana, where over $20 million was won by a group of high rollers over the span of a few days. These were rumored to be the work of a team of sequential trackers.

As I have shown, sizable wins cannot be chalked up by card-counting techniques in a short space of time. Nor is it plausible to suspect that these players were cheats, since scrutiny of the players at such high stakes is very intense. For players consistently betting more than $1,000 a hand, it would be as difficult to pull off a cheating scam such as this as it would be to rob a bank if the police had advance knowledge of it. Nor could their wins have simply been luck, since their bets were small compared to the total of their winnings.

This motivated me to return to my analysis. It occurred to me that my research had been based on the assumption that when I predicted a certain card would appear within the next six cards, I meant it would do so with "equiprobability," i.e., that there was just as likely to be three cards as six cards separating the signature card from the key card. This is not in fact the case. It's almost twice as likely that there will be one card separating the signature card from the target card, as that the signature card will immediately follow the target card. There is slightly less chance that there will be a 2-card separation than a one-card, and again, slightly less chance that there will be a three-card separation than a two-card separation, and so on, until we get to the seventh card, when the odds our target card will appear are the same as if the shuffle had been truly unpredictable. The difference between the likelihoods of the card turning up in each position may make the method workable after all.

My studies were based on a computer software model. I am not yet entirely certain that the computer model correctly simulates the actual range of casino shuffles correctly, especially since I had not programmed the model myself. In any case, I'm sure a lot of my readers would not believe it even if I did, since a good deal of traveling would be involved in acquiring the data!

In Stanford Wong's *Professional Blackjack* (1994), however, there is a study of an actual casino-style shuffle performed by an ex-dealer. Using one deck, the dealer shuffled the cards in a riffle-riffle-strip-riffle action, which is not dissimilar to many mini-baccarat shuffles. Ten total shuffles were performed. Every card was noted down as it was dealt. Wong discovered that after the shuffle, cards that were next to each other before the shuffle were separated by one to six cards 47 percent of the time. This couldn't reasonably be attributed to chance, and is pretty much conclusive evidence that card location works.

Wong gave figures on the number of gaps between cards. There were twenty-three occasions in which two-card sequences retained their order. There were fifty-seven instances in which one card separated initially adjacent cards, forty with a two-card separation, forty-three for three cards, thirty-five for four cards, twenty-three for five cards, and eighteen for six cards. Wong's study is not directly applicable to baccarat, because baccarat is played with six decks rather than one. Our prediction, however, should be more accurate than Wong's data suggests, since it is harder to randomize six or eight decks than it is to randomize one. In any case, Wong's data has results very close to my own computer-generated results.

This indicates an imbalance which may favor one bet or the other to a small degree. For example, say you see the 9 of Spades, the 6 of Clubs, the Jack of Hearts, and the 9 of Clubs come out before the shuffle. Then you see the 9 of Spades after the shuffle, closely followed by the 6 of Clubs and the Jack of Hearts. The Jack of Hearts is followed by the 5 of Hearts, i.e., it is not our target card. Looking at the above Wong data, we can see that it is 25 percent more likely that the 9 of Clubs will be in the player's first two cards (the first and third card dealt) than the banker's first two cards. This should give the player hand a diluted but still significant advantage.

Ideally, a player could play through a mini-baccarat shoe noting down the two cards preceding every 9 and use this information to determine when a 9 would be more likely to appear in the bank or player hand. He could then raise his bet knowing he had the advantage over the house. Of course, this depends on the particular shuffle, no two of which are exactly alike. If you think you have located an exploitable game, play with a particular dealer through five shoes of mini-baccarat, and note down the order of the cards as they are dealt from each shuffled pack. If groups of adjacent cards tend to remain close together after the shuffle, this should be fairly obvious.

Teams of professional blackjack players typically use a ruse involving a high roller with a woman on each arm to make bets in a casino. The high roller will count down the deck while the women, known as "key-card girls," memorize sequences of cards. The reasons for this are twofold: this looks natural and provides good cover, and three players can utilize information more easily than one. The high roller could note down the cards as they are dealt using the composition-dependent strategy mentioned earlier, while one girl could track sequences of 8s and the other could track sequences of 9s.

I recently became aware of another sequential tracking method used at blackjack which involves memorizing a sequence of twelve cards. The idea is not to predict the occurrence of a specific card, but to get some idea of the composition of a hand. The blackjack player is limited to twelve card sequences because of the limitations of human memory. If he wanted, the baccarat player could, with the aid of the pencils and scorecard provided, note down the entire sequence of cards in the preshuffled pack. If the shuffle is sloppy enough, it seems likely that a player could, as was apparently done in chemin de fer so many years ago, predict the result of entire hands. With a one-pass shuffle, computer-perfect calculations reliably predict the value of *every single card!*

Consequently, sequential tracking is a simplification of what might be described as "computer-perfect" tracking, which would involve a precise analysis of the transition (the exact movement of each card) of shuffle states. Of course, it's not quite that simple. The computational difficulty in trying to predict every six-card sequence is a very complex matter. Also, every shuffle will be different.

If you were to attempt this very difficult task, I would note the value of every card, and note the composition of hands preceding four-card ties, such as 10 of Spades (player), 6 of Clubs (banker), 6 of Spades (player), and Queen of Hearts (banker). If you knew the cards that were dealt in the hand previous to this one, you could watch for them after the shuffle and place a large wager on the tie bet when these cards come out in a sequence. Note that it doesn't matter if our prediction is a little off, as it will be most of the time. It doesn't matter if the new order of the four cards was 6 of Clubs, 10 of Spades, Queen of Hearts, and 6 of Spades, it's still a win for the tie. If the two 10s get lost in the shuffle, we still have a large advantage over the house on the tie wager, provided those two 6s are in the hand. Even one 6 alone, or the two 10s, will reduce the house edge to quite a low level.

Using either technique to analyze shuffles, you should be aware that knowledge of the undealt cards will significantly improve your card prediction. If there have been twelve cards dealt and your signature cards come out, then there is quite a strong likelihood that the signature and target cards have been split apart, and the target card is, in fact, somewhere else in the pack. If there are only twelve cards remaining in the shoe, however, then you know that the signature cards and target cards are close together, because you have seen the rest of the pack dealt out. Currently the MGM, the Las Vegas Hilton, and the Mirage casinos all use a single-riffle, one-pass shuffle.

The following chart gives data on the impact on the odds of various bets when you know a certain card will appear. It can be used for sequential tracking or other advantage-play techniques detailed in the next chapter. The figures assume your knowledge of the appearance of a card is 100 percent accurate.

First or Third Card	Banker Hand Expectation	Player Hand Expectation
Ace	5.36%	−7.83%
2	4.91	−7.36
3	4.28	−6.72
4	3.23	−5.62
5	1.13	−3.47
6	−2.97	0.76
7	−9.41	7.37
8	−19.12	17.29
9	−23.25	21.53
0	5.52	−7.99

Second or Fourth Card

Ace	−7.25	5.10
2	−6.54	4.38
3	−5.89	3.71
4	−4.69	2.48
5	−2.05	0.22
6	0.42	−2.72
7	6.83	−9.29
8	16.49	−19.23
9	20.64	−23.49
0	−7.93	5.80

Fifth Card

Ace	3.48	−5.88
2	−4.77	2.61
3	−12.64	10.68
4	−20.09	18.32
5	−15.63	13.74
6	−11.02	9.02
7	−6.38	4.25
8	−1.24	−1.11
9	3.53	−5.99
0	12.75	−15.43

Sixth Card

Ace	−7.86	5.76
2	−0.47	−1.82
3	6.84	−9.93
4	11.92	−14.55
5	14.51	−17.22
6	14.42	−17.14
7	8.60	−11.16
8	2.21	−4.60
9	−3.71	1.48
0	−15.05	13.13

Figures assume a six-deck shoe, 5 percent bank commission. Figures for eight decks will show slightly improved expectation for the player and reduced expectation for the bank for the reasons mentioned elsewhere.

No figures for the tie bet are given, as knowledge of any *one* card does not offer us any favorable bets on this wager.

For a more comprehensive study of the probability distributions when a card is known, see George Joseph's *The Effect of Marked Cards on a Baccarat Game,* available from the Gamblers Book Club.

Shuffle-Spooking

Another lucrative, and hitherto unpublished winning technique, is one I call "shuffle-spooking." It is derived from a technique poker cheats use, though its use at baccarat is both legal and ethical under my interpretation of Nevada and Atlantic City statutes. It will be of particular interest to players with $20/20$ vision. Like the previous methods mentioned, you track the shuffle, but this time you do it physically.

Sit to the immediate left or right of the main croupier. These seats are usually unpopular because of their uncomfortably close proximity to casino personnel. Take one, though, because with some dealers (approximately 20 percent) you can often see cards in the shuffle and trace them to where they are dealt. Often dealers arch the cards so high on the riffle that you can see them pass by. Though they will be traveling at a very high speed, it is possible to note the location of a card.

It is easier to determine the presence of face cards, because the pictures register with your eye much more quickly than the numbers on other cards. Since you will only see part of the individual cards as they are shuffled, you should practice recognizing cards by taking a deck of your own and blocking off areas of the card with your hand until you became familiar with its truncated appearance. If you can enhance this aspect of your perception, you will be able to spook the shuffle without looking at it directly, which makes this technique very hard to detect. As an alternative method, it is often helpful to wear a peaked cap or dark glasses to hide your attention to the shuffle, which the majority of ordinary players take no interest in.

Skilled card players develop the ability to replay past events in the mind's eye; this is known as tacheoscopic vision. This is a very useful ability to use in shuffle-spooking. Specialist computer software exists to develop this skill.

Another exploitable vulnerability in the shuffle exists in some casinos where a cut-card is used to cut off a fixed number of cards, usually fourteen, and one more hand is dealt when the cut-card comes out. This is the house procedure in many American riverboat casinos and in countries such as Australia. The dealer puts one cut-card at the bottom of the deck and another more than fourteen cards above it, say fifteen to twenty. He removes this segment from the pack and puts it on the table. As the dealer lifts the clump, he will expose the card on the back to anyone standing immediately behind the dealer. An agent can signal the value of this card to a player immediately in front of the dealer. The front player counts the number of cards in the segment. This isn't difficult, as the dealer will insert the cut-card fourteen cards from the bottom, although the front player will have only a second or two to do this. You will then know how many cards separate the bottom of the deck from the card at the bottom of the stack.

Then all that is required is to count down from 416 (or 312 in a six-deck game), betting the table minimum on the banker, till you know the card you have spotted is about to be played. You can then place a large bet on whatever wager is favored by that card.

Sometimes, the front player will have the opportunity to know the value of more than just one card. Some dealers stick the cut-card in at a 45-degree angle and lift up several cards. Again, this happens in an instant, but the perceptive player will be able to spot the value of several cards and anticipate their appearance when the cut-card comes out on the last hand of the deck. If you know two or three cards will appear, your advantage is frequently over 100 percent, and you may be able to make wagers on more than one bet.

A variant on shuffle-spooking can sometimes be used at the mini-baccarat table. In this case, a player should sink low in his seat while watching the shuffle. As the dealer splits the pack and places the decks on top of one another, a player may able to see the bottom card of each segment as it is dropped. He can then have a good idea of when that card is to be dealt. This assumes, of course, that the dealer breaks the pack into even segments, otherwise the prediction will be too rough. This requires a skillful dealer. You should note the average number of cards in a segment while using this method.

With more than a hand's worth of error, the segments will be too uneven to give you useful information. If this is, indeed, the case, try obtaining the cut-card and aim for the approximate position of the card you have seen which gives you the greatest advantage. Locate the line of least resistance in this area by applying gentle pressure, and you will find that the natural break in the deck will allow you to locate the desired card with 100 percent accuracy.

It is much easier to perform this task if you use a good act, such as that of an inebriated drunk who slouches low in his chair, unable to sit any straighter. This will allow you a better view than you could normally attain and will draw the heat off you, as the casino personnel are unlikely to take notice of one more drunk. Some players have been known to use wheelchairs to achieve a similar effect. There are many other ploys for "hanging low" without arousing suspicion, but I'll leave these to your imagination.

It will be helpful to use a relay while shuffle-spooking. You can signal to a partner on the other side of the table to make a large bet on whichever hand the card distribution favors. There are two main advantages to this: first, the house is less likely to catch on to what you're doing and take countermeasures; second, many dealers "tighten up" their shuffling technique if a player is making large bets next to them, subconsciously protecting the cards.

In theory, a player could combine card-counting with shuffle-spooking. Then, in theory, he could gain a larger edge by combining knowledge of the position of a card with knowledge of the undealt cards. We can illustrate this by the results of analysis showing that to have a 9 as the first player card in a deck without any 10s puts the player at a 10 percent disadvantage, which is considerably less than the more-than-21 percent advantage the player would enjoy with a standard deck. A player who knew there were no 10s in the deck would not bet on the player and save himself from making a bad wager. With twice as many

10s as normally in the deck, the player advantage is almost 40 percent. The player who doesn't know that an excess of 10s remains underestimates his advantage and bets too conservatively. This illustrates the potential of pooling the information given by the two systems. The considerable analysis necessary to develop this concept further is a task left to the interested reader. Limited simulations show that it is unlikely to be worthwhile unless you know an 8 or 9 will appear in a certain hand near the very end of the pack.

Dealers who expose cards while shuffling are generally less experienced and proficient than those who do not. When searching for favorable opportunities, it is often helpful to concentrate on casinos which are introducing a new batch of dealers. In Nevada, during the summer tourist season many casinos are forced to use inadequately trained temporary staff to cope with demand.

5

Other Advantage-Play Techniques

Other techniques exist to give the player knowledge of when a particular card is to be dealt.

Warping

In casinos where the cards are not changed regularly, the cards will get bent, cut, and generally beat-up after a few hours use. The cards develop "warps" from players handling them and can even be torn. The card edges can get frayed from being dragged along the surface of the felt by the dealer, which eventually causes them to split into layers. The physical condition of the cards can also deteriorate rapidly in humid climates. Sometimes, cards are simply manufactured with some slight defect.

An observant player can use this knowledge to his advantage if he notices the back of a card has nonuniform characteristics as it is waiting to be dealt. Note, this is not the same as playing with marked cards, which is illegal. The player is merely taking advantage of the game conditions as they are offered.

Card-Steering

Often a player in a position seated to the far right or far left of the dealer can spot the card at the bottom of the pile as it is shuffled. If he can get the cut-card he can cut this card to the top, or if another player performs this action, he may able to estimate the number of cards before it appears. Some casinos are alert to this technique and specify a minimum number of cards to be cut from the top or bottom of the deck. This technique can be very lucrative; if you bet ten times your average bank bet on whatever wager is favored by the first card, you can average a profit on an entire six-deck shoe. The proviso is that you need to practice the technique until you can perform it with near 100 percent accuracy. It is helpful to take a deck of cards, remove half a deck, or less, at random, and attempt to estimate the precise number of cards remaining. You should practice until you can do this nineteen times out of twenty with no error. You must be able to predict exactly when this card will come up more than 50 percent of the time or you will have no advantage at all.

After the bottom card has been dealt, assuming you are using no other advantage-play technique, you should leave the table. Of course, if you persistently leave the table after the first few hands you may attract attention, so sometimes it may be wise to play deeper into the deck for cover purposes. It is best to play with 100 percent control of the cut-card, so a player should either try to find a heads-up game or play with a team who can occupy all the available seats.

The Nevada courts have explicitly stated that it is not illegal for a player to take advantage of a dealer's sloppiness. There is nothing to prevent a player taking advantage of this information or signaling it (surreptitiously or otherwise) to a confederate. This is usually the case in other jurisdictions as well.

Another angle on card-steering involves recording every card that is dealt. When there are one to six cards remaining, sometimes these cards will be put into the discard pile, then placed at the bottom of the stack as the dealer shuffles. Often he will grab the bottom of the stack and accidentally crimp this bottom segment. Try to follow the bottom cards through the shuffle. As with shuffle-spooking, it is normally beyond human judgment to do this with 100 percent accuracy, though, the natural break in the deck, combined with the crimp, which creates an air pocket with this segment of cards, means that if you obtain the cut-card, you will tend to cut to the end of this group, much as an old book repeatedly opens at the same page. Again, locate the line of least resistance and drag the cut-card back by a couple of millimeters, or about one-tenth of an inch. You should then be able to predict the subsequent cards to be dealt.

This technique requires some practice and the availability of a game where the dealer has a fairly sloppy way of shuffling; it is likely that you will only find these conditions at mini-baccarat. You should try mimicking the dealer's shuffle style on your kitchen table (there is no need to do this as skillfully as the dealer) and practicing cutting to the start of the bottom segment. If you can do this with even a small chance of success, you can have a huge edge; then you can usually predict the outcome of the hand with near certainty. This is particularly the case when you know a pair of high-valued cards are going to come out; you can then place a wager on the tie, with its attractive 8 to 1 payoff.

It is essential to keep meticulous records on any dealer whose shuffling style betrays any vulnerability. Such details should include: physical description, the casino where he works, his shift, and what seat best exposes his weakness. When playing any dealer, however, use discretion.

If you play with only one specific dealer and win consistently, the casino will become suspicious, so try to play with other dealers for cover. Watch the amounts other players win and lose during a single session. You should get some idea of what the pit boss is used to in terms of players' winnings that arise purely from good fortune. Never go on playing if your winnings threaten to overtake what could be reasonably attributed to luck.

Coupons

To encourage further play at the tables, casinos will often offer free "match-play" coupons or chips (there is no practical difference between the two). These allow you to make a no-lose wager at the casino game of your choice. This is free money, so take it! When you use the freebie you must place a wager equivalent to its value alongside it, e.g., if the match-play is worth $10, you must put $10 of your own money down beside it.

Sometimes the casino will not allow you to put the chip on any wager which does not pay 1 to 1, which disqualifies both the banker and tie bets (it's not a good idea to put it on the tie anyway). If you lose your bet, they take your money and your coupon. If you win, they pay you the value of your money bet plus the value of the coupon, which is still taken away from you. If there is a push, no money changes hands and your coupon is not taken.

If you use a coupon at baccarat, it is easy to calculate its value. If you bet on the player, it is simply half the value of the coupon minus the house edge, so a five-dollar coupon is worth $2.45 if you bet on the player or the banker.

You will often find people wary of using coupons for a variety of reasons. These are mostly tour parties who want to stick with the slot machines. By all means, hustle them for all they are worth. The advanced practitioners of "couponomy" can earn as much as $20 a day by seeking out the best deals. Hardly a fortune, but a significant amount for the average low-stakes mini-baccarat player. Occasionally, you will find something just a little more juicy.

Baccarat is not necessarily the best place to use a coupon, since skilled blackjack and craps players can get slightly more value from their coupons. The difference, however, is so small as to be irrelevant, probably no more than a few cents worth. If you are allowed to bet on the banker and the commission is not subtracted with a coupon, then the bank bet is decidedly the best wager in the casino on which to use your freebie, as this gives you an edge of 1.23 percent over the house. You are, of course, still paying 5 percent "vig" on your regular bet, so the wager is effectively a break-even.

There is a strategy that two players can take advantage of to maximize the value of their coupons. Ordinarily you are not allowed to hedge bets by placing your match-play on the bank and real money on the player; this would give you either a push or a win, and therefore no possibility of a loss. With a partner, however, you can hedge coupons, or a coupon and money, and split any profits afterward. Your expectation would be slightly higher if you both made wagers on the bank, but it's worthwhile giving up a few cents in expectation in order to guarantee you can, at worst, push. Another tactic is to avoid placing a bet alongside your coupon by placing it alongside someone else's bet. This is easy to do if you have a friend at the table who is already gambling, but it requires guts to approach a complete stranger. The house doesn't really approve of this.

Another factor to consider is whether the coupon counts toward the table minimum. If there is a ten-dollar minimum and you have a five-dollar coupon, then the advantage of the coupon will be diluted if you have to bet $10 as well as the coupon in order to make a minimum bet.

The glamorous life of coupon hustler involves an uncanny ability to hunt down their prey. They will scour the gambling magazines (not the ones the pros read, the glossy casino-approved ones totally lacking in substance) for freebies. They will make sure their name appears on every casino mailing list (this will ensure a tidal wave of junk mail through the door every day). They also have a wide network of low-level pit personnel and fellow gamblers to help them seek out the best deals.

6

Cheating

Unusual for a casino card game, the baccarat player is virtually immune from being cheated by the house. This is because of the structure of the game. The game is not a straight adversarial confrontation between the house and the player. Most of the money is dealt on the main part of the game, the banker or player bets. If this amount is divided approximately equally between the banker or player, the casino would have no incentive to cheat, since it would merely be favoring one side over the other, with its gains canceling its losses.

With a single player, such as a high roller, cheating would have to be done after the player had placed his bet, since most players will switch between player and bank intermittently. The standard tricks of cardsharps, such as dealing seconds, are designed for handheld single-deck games and are not easily transferable to shoe games. One method that could be used to cheat the player involves a specially made dealing box which delivers cards to the dealer through a slit in its side when tapped. This can be done surreptitiously to give the player up to nine cards when there is a large bet on the banker. While such devices were common in the 1950s and 1960s, I think it's highly unlikely that one would be found today, as it would constitute prima facie evidence of cheating. In the United States of America, the greatly increased powers of various gaming control bodies have in any case restricted, though not eliminated, the prevalence of cheating.

If a player were to detect cheating in any form, there is a simple winning method to exploit it. When a large bet is placed on the bank, place a small wager on the player, and vice versa. If your suspicions are correct, the odds of the game will be working in your favor. I seriously doubt that you will detect any cheating at baccarat, however. Extensive research has not revealed any recorded case of cheating at baccarat by the house in the last twenty years.

While a player is unlikely to be parted from his cash through some underhand method used at the tables, there are, of course, far more simple and brutal methods to part a man from his money. Generally speaking, you are not particularly at risk from crime in a casino area, but Nevada, particularly, has less crime than many other American jurisdictions. Nevertheless, criminals looking for a quick score are disproportionately likely to go after a man who plays baccarat rather than a keno or slot player. Stories of gamblers being mugged after a big win have certain human-interest value and are widely reported, which tends to blow such occurrences out of proportion, but it is a real tragedy for the individual concerned.

To protect oneself, it's best to never travel in or out of the casino alone. Be especially cautious if you have a long winning streak. If you were a thief, what would you do? Mug tourists at random or go after the guy at the baccarat table who decides to quit after winning ten hands in a row? If you feel you're being watched, ask the pit personnel if there's another exit you can use.

Here's a trick I learned from a fellow professional to protect yourself. Take an old wallet and some dead credit cards, cutting your name and any identifying information off them. Add some business cards, passport photos, and any other miscellaneous junk you can think of. Put twenty single dollar bills into the wallet. This makes it look very inviting, and you can use this money for incidental expenses. You want everyone to think your real cash comes from the wallet, whereas it is actually stored in several locations around your person where a mugger would be less likely to look, such as an inside pocket.

When you buy in for chips at the cashier cage, "palm" your real dollars, i.e., unobtrusively remove them hidden in the palm of your hand, then make a show of reaching for your wallet and pretending to extract your money. When cashing out, take the wallet out, motion that you're putting your winnings inside, but palm the folded bills. Then put your wallet in your hip pocket, and as you turn away from the cage, put your real money in your coat pocket while anyone checking you out is on your blind side.

Obviously, the intention is for the thief to steal your fake wallet without taking anything further from you, only to discover his mistake later. This will not prevent you from being assaulted, or even save you from having all your cash taken in every case, but most criminals can't afford the time to be thorough.

You should always keep any money not essential for expenses or necessary for lasting the gambling session back in your hotel room, hence the importance of determining how much money you should take with you to the casino (see Chapter 2). This is not only to avoid crime, but also temptation for yourself.

While inside the casino, the player's bankroll is fairly safe from standard card-cheating practices, but the same cannot be said of cheating by other players. Cheats at baccarat mainly use illegal methods to determine which card will be subsequently dealt. An exception to this is a technique known as "past-posting," whereby a cheat will increase the amount of his bet after he has already won a hand. It takes a great deal of skill to do this unobserved by either the dealer, the pit personnel, or the video surveillance, and is generally undertaken only by an expert.

One method to predict the value of the first card is an illegal variant of bottom-steering, whereby the player sits down at an unoccupied table, is given the cut-card, and stabs it into the pack, twisting it so he can see the denomination of the card at that point in the deck. If it is a good card he will know that the player has a good chance of success; if it is bad, the banker will be favored. If it is neutral, he will remove the cut-card and search for another card elsewhere in the deck. He then places a large bet on the option favored by the first card.

A simple method preferred by sleight-of-hand artists is known as hand-mucking. The cheat conceals cards in his sleeves, sits down at the baccarat table waiting till no eyes are on him, places a large bet, and switches his cards for the ones he has been dealt.

A "dauber" physically marks the back of certain cards with small quantities of paint on his fingers. He can then tell when they are going to appear in the future. Because this technique is often easily detected, some clever daubers pioneered a technique using ultraviolet paint (which is normally invisible to the naked eye) and ultraviolet contact lenses. Because of this ingenious method, most casinos, in their formidable array of game-protection devices, now have surveillance equipment which can detect ultraviolet.

A "crimper" puts a very slight bend on the corners of cards he wants to remember for the purposes of future recognition. Players tend to mangle cards anyway without any malicious intent. For this reason, and to prevent the use of the above methods, many casinos will introduce new cards at the beginning of every shoe.

"Peeking" involves collusion between a dealer and player when the dealer pulls the first card halfway out of the shoe and flashes the corner to a player across the table, who bets accordingly. Sometimes the dealer is sloppy and does this without realizing it. With or without dealer compliance, the player has only a split second to get his bet down.

Dealer Errors

Especially clever players can induce mispays by inexperienced dealers. One little known but effective technique is to bet an identical amount of multiple chips for several hands, then unobtrusively slip a higher denomination chip on the bottom hand. Should the player lose, the chances are that the dealer will not notice the bottom chip and fail to separate it from those of lower denomination. The player then bets a large amount of lower-denomination chips, preferably on several boxes, in the hope that should these bets win, the dealer will reach into his rack and return the higher denomination chip.

Naturally, it helps to look for dealers nearing the end of a graveyard shift who seem either fatigued or inexperienced. Of course, sometimes dealers make errors without any help from the player. An acquaintance of mine once received an Ace and a 10 as his first two cards, and was somewhat surprised when the dealer took the cards from him and paid three to two on his bet; he would have been less surprised if he had actually been playing not baccarat but blackjack, for which this would have been the appropriate response. Anyway, my friend wasn't confident enough to inform the dealer of his awareness that they were playing two different games, and so he humbly accepted the payment.

Dealer errors just as frequently help as hinder the player, and there is no reason why a player should not be selective about the mistakes he chooses to point out. Because he is the one risking the money, he should be more alert to any mistakes, while the dealer is likely to be bored to tears by the repetitive nature of his job. On the other hand, other players at the table tend to point out mistakes which would be in the house's favor, while tactfully ignoring those made to the benefit of a fellow player. For this reason, the player's real-life expectation is probably slightly higher than the figures presented in Chapter 1. If you watch games of baccarat closely over several months, you will notice mistakes that amount to several hundred or even several thousand dollars over this period. One mistake an hour in your favor will wipe out the casino's edge.

One simple method which could be used to cheat the unobservant player is for the croupier to depart from the fixed dealing rules in order to favor one side or the other. For this reason, all players should have a good working knowledge of the mechanics of the drawing-and-standing decisions. Should the dealer accidentally favor the bet you have wagered on, the net effect on your expectation will be fairly negligible provided these mistakes are not systematic and not too blatant (e.g., banker standing on 0).

If a croupier should accidentally deal a card contrary to the drawing-and-standing rules, and this mistake is pointed out to him or he realizes his mistake, then a common practice is to put this card under the shoe for dealing as the first card of the next hand. You can exploit this information for betting purposes exactly as you would with bottom-steering. This is an especially valuable dealer error. Again, this requires you to fully understand the game in order to spot any mistake.

Note that the legal position of a dealer who flashes a card, or a dealer who makes an error, depends on exactly what took place. A player who exposes his cards accidentally while dealing is not committing any crime, nor is anyone who takes advantage of this information. It is the casino's responsibility to make sure that all bets have been placed before any cards are exposed. Any collusion between two players has to be proven. A player is under no responsibility to draw attention to any payoff errors. Even if the player is using a technique to induce a payoff error such as the one above, the casino can do little about it, since a player may simply enjoy betting his money in an unusual manner. Be aware, however, that you have no right to keep an overpayment, should it be detected by casino personnel. Also be aware that any scheme involving collusion between players and dealers is by its very nature perilous and subject to the full retribution of the law.

There have been several recorded instances of marked-card teams operating in Las Vegas in the last few years. Undoubtedly, this is because of the higher stakes that are played for in baccarat. Marked-card scams are mathematically much less advantageous than at other card games. For example, in baccarat, the most valuable card to have knowledge of is the 9, but this will only give you a 21 percent edge if you know it is the first card to be dealt. By comparison, the most valuable card to have foreknowledge of in blackjack is the Ace, which gives you a 52 percent advantage in equivalent circumstances.

A recent scam involving collusion between players and dealers was chronicled in the *Las Vegas Review Journal*. This group, involving three dealers, had taken more than $700,000 through a "false shuffle" scheme from three casinos, the Sheraton Desert Inn, the MGM Grand Hotel, and the Las Vegas Hilton. The dealers in mini-baccarat games faked shuffling the cards, a technique which is part of the standard inventory of magicians and card cheats. The players determined which cards would be dealt and bet accordingly. Their crimes took place between April and June 1995. Bill Zender, author of *Cheating for the Casino Executive*, testified for the prosecution, stating, "the cards that appeared before the shuffle reappeared in reverse order."

Like most criminals, the team got caught because they got greedy. It would only have been necessary to preserve the order of three or four hands through the shuffle to gain a huge advantage, even if the players bet the same amount on every hand. Such a scheme would be very difficult to detect, and virtually impossible to prosecute successfully, since the perpetrators could claim, with some justification, that they were merely exploiting the sloppy shuffling of the dealer, which is not a crime in itself, using the sequential tracking methods mentioned earlier.

Lastly, in this book, you may have noticed the absence of the customary preliminary paragraph explaining that the author intends his knowledge of cheating to be used for educational purposes only and that he does not condone its use. You won't find that kind of coy moralizing from me. The casino industry pretends to be purely for entertainment, yet it will happily take the last dollar of working men with families to feed, who are driven to ruin by deep psychological problems. The industry is no better and no worse than the proposition-bet hustler who makes his money by duping ordinary people into making a wager that is apparently favorable, yet actually works to the hustler's advantage. Millions of people descend on Las Vegas every year in the belief that they have a magic system to beat the casinos, yet most will see their hard-earned savings quickly dissipated at the tables. Therefore, should the casino industry find itself on the wrong end of a scam, in my opinion it deserves everything it gets. Anyone who has a problem with this kind of "blood-sport" attitude should consider doing something about Nevada's teen suicide rate before shedding tears over a fractional loss of the gambling industry's profits.

Nevertheless, I don't advise anyone to become a cheat. Cheating is a highly skilled profession, and mastery of some of the techniques involved takes years. The information given here doesn't even scratch the surface. Once versed in these black arts, you must overcome an army of casino staff and state-of-the-art surveillance equipment in order to succeed, and should you fail, you risk the most severe penalties. The risks simply outweigh the potential gain.

A word of warning: if you cheat, or even if you win money quite legitimately at baccarat through one of the techniques here, be aware that you will probably come to the attention of the Griffin detective agency. This sinister and probably unconstitutional organization serves to protect the casinos of the world, but particularly those in Nevada and Atlantic City, from those gamblers who play with a long-term advantage. They monitor casinos directly from their own offices (they have a television link to camera surveillance). They are highly skilled in detecting methods of cheating, though they are less knowledgeable of advantage-play techniques. If you win a lot of money persistently from a casino that uses Griffin, you will end up in the "Griffin Mug Book," a computerized database of faces and personal details. They can cross-reference this database with any surveillance footage in a few seconds. Being in the mug book is a little like being on a credit blacklist. You will find you are denied entry to many of the casinos of the world. In some cases, the Griffin agency has been known to use illegal methods to obtain results, and has been responsible for the hospitalization of some individuals. Doubtless the organization would have been broken up long ago were it not for the fine work it does protecting state gaming revenues.

7

Chemin de Fer

Chemin de fer is a French game, popular in Europe, particularly in France and Monte Carlo. It was introduced into the United States in the 1920s but never really caught on, and was gradually replaced by the rise of Punto Banco, which became the only form of American baccarat. Recently however, the larger casinos such as the Trump Taj Mahal in Atlantic City have offered the game, suggesting that this interesting elder variation of baccarat may be making something of a comeback.

Also known by its nickname Chimmy, the main difference between this form of baccarat and the others is that the house is not directly involved, and players have the opportunity to hold the bank. The house derives its edge from a tax on the banker; the casino will take 5 percent of all winning banker bets when the shoe has been dealt out.

Typically, seven to twelve players are involved. The first banker is the player who puts up the highest stake. He gets the shoe and continues to deal and hold the shoe until he loses a hand. Then the next player on the right will receive the bank. The bank, therefore, rotates around the table, which gave the game its name (literally meaning "railway"). The player receiving the bank is required to put up a stake not less than the previous banker. A player may decline the bank by declaring "*la banque passe.*" The bank then passes to the nearest player on the right.

The banker then places his wager onto a front area of the table layout (or a croupier may do this for him). Then, beginning with the individual on the banker's right, the other players place their wagers in numbered boxes in front of them. The combined total of the players' wagers is not allowed to exceed that of the banker's. If the total wagers of the players is less than that of the banker, then the banker (or croupier) adjusts his stake accordingly.

Any player may cover the entire bank by calling out, "*Banco!*" If this happens, all other players' wagers are removed. A player may also call out, "*banco suivi!*" (banco continued) which means that if that player loses a hand he is given preference over all other players in covering the entire bank on the succeeding hand. A player who declares, "*banco suivi,*" effectively freezes out other players and will not be very popular if he does this for very long. Many casinos also offer the player the chance to cover half the bank by calling, "*Demi-banco.*"

Play then proceeds exactly as in American-style baccarat, with two cards dealt to the player, who is the individual wagering the largest amount of money against the bank, and two cards to the banker. These cards are dealt face down and their totals added, and no total can exceed 9. If a total of 8 or 9 is declared immediately, wagers are settled. Unlike American-style baccarat, however, the player is allowed to decide whether to draw or stand on a total of 5. As with the American game, other player options are restricted: he must draw with a total between 1 and 4 and stand with a 6 or 7. The highest total wins, and ties are declared a standoff, in which no money changes hands.

The degree of freedom the banker is given is usually also limited. However, on the assumption that the banker has completely free choice as to whether he draws or stands, the best strategies for both sides are given in the next sections.

The Player's Best Strategy

The player's only option is whether to draw or stand on a total of 5. Perceptive readers will recognize that there are four cards which could help the player, and five cards that hinder, while 10-valued cards leave things as they are. It would therefore seem logical to stand, although it's a more complicated issue than that. This is because if a player always stands or always draws, he effectively reveals his hand to the banker. Therefore, to keep the banker guessing, he must often bluff, i.e., make a decision against the odds in order to fool the banker, much as poker players do. The player's best strategy has been calculated to draw with a frequency of nine times in eleven and stand with a frequency of two times in eleven. This can be approximated as drawing 80 percent of the time. You must try to avoid doing this in a pattern, because, obviously, if you always draw the first four times you hold a total of five and then stand, then draw another four times, and so on, your strategy will soon become apparent to the banker. To make your drawing-and-standing frequency as unpredictable as possible, try looking quickly at the second hand of your watch: if forty-eight seconds or more have elapsed, then stay; otherwise draw. The banker also needs to bluff on occasion.

The Banker's Best Strategy

The banker's strategy is more complex because of his greater number of options:

If His Count Is	Action
0, 1, 2	Draw
3	Stay if the player draws on 8, otherwise draw
4	Stand if the player draws on 1, 8, 9, 10; draw if the player stands or draws on 2 through 7
5	Stand if the player draws on 1 to 3 or 8 to 10; draw if the player stands or draws on 4 through 7
6	Stay if the player draws on 1 to 5 or 8 to 10, a probability of 1,429/2,288 (approx. 60 percent) if the player stays. Draw if the player draws on 6 or 7, a probability of 859/2,288 (approx. 40 percent) if the player stays.
7	Stay

The rules given here are not necessarily standard. Often the casino will not allow the banker unlimited choice. Sometimes the player is allowed other options. With this approach, however, and with both players following the best strategy, the player loses at the rate of 1.37 percent. Because of the 5 percent charge on winning bets, the banker loses at the rate of 1.16 percent.

Chemin de fer can be a very exciting and tense game to play, owing to the amount of risk the banker must take on. The banker cannot skim off the profits of a series of winning hands and play with the balance; he has to continue putting up the entire value of the bank. If the bank is faded, the amount risked will double. This means a player who begins by putting up $500 will end up betting $8,000 after four successive wins. As long as the players keep fading, this amount will increase until the banker voluntarily relinquishes the bank.

Naturally, this sort of dramatic increase in stakes is not for the faint-hearted. Some people might consider it quite enough excitement to be betting a few thousand dollars, let alone have their stake doubled, quadrupled, and octupled! Nevertheless, it is the nearest thing to a roller-coaster adrenaline fix you will get in a casino.

Some casinos give the banker the option of cutting the bank total in half after three successive wins. This gives the banker the chance to come away with a profit even if the bank hand loses the fourth coup.

Note the similarity between the successive doubling of the bank's stake and the anti-Martingale system mentioned in Chapter 2. Like an anti-Martingale bettor, the banker will find he has a series of comparatively small wins punctuated by winning streaks of dazzling brilliance. This is fine if you wish to experience gambling at its greatest intensity, but it is also a very dangerous game for the inadequately financed player.

Until quite recently, it was still possible to find chemin de fer in many of the finer English casinos. The English version of the game was of considerably more interest to knowledgeable players than the Continental version, because rather than a fixed percentage of the winnings, the club took its profit from a table charge per hour. In this version of the game, the banker plays with a long-run advantage. A player could make consistent profits by following the correct strategy and betting as little as possible on the player, and as much as his bankroll would sensibly allow as the banker. Most other players would realize, intuitively, that the bank had the advantage, but their natural conservatism prevented them from frequently holding the bank, as this requires a great deal of capital risk. Unfortunately, in England the game has largely been replaced by Punto Banco. If you should find a version where a table charge is made, it should be fairly easy to make profits if you have a large bankroll.

The passing of the game in England is, to my mind, a minor tragedy. So much of the history of the London casino establishment is owed to the game. Clubs such as Aspinalls made both their name and reputation on chemin de fer. The replacement of the game by Punto Banco was clearly a financial decision on the part of the casinos rather than one inflicted by the will of the public. The game was still popular, but earned less for the house than Punto Banco, because, for obvious reasons, people will gamble away a larger sum of money in an hour than they are willing to pay as a flat tax.

Card-Counting at Chemin de Fer

The only published study I am aware of about the potential of card-counting strategies on chemin de fer was by Downton and Lockwood in an article entitled "Computer Studies of Baccarat" (*Journal of the Royal Statistical Association*, 1975). They tried adding and removing various combinations of cards from the shoe in various computer calculations without finding a situation in which the player had an advantage. The closest they came was when the deck contained an extra forty-eight 10s and no 5s, 6s, 7s, or 8s. They concluded that an excess of 10s and 4s seems to favor the player, as does a lack of 6s and 7s.

In the light of the work that has been done on American-style baccarat this is hardly surprising, since as far as the player is concerned the rules are very similar, and we have already seen that no worthwhile counting strategy exists for the player in the modern game.

The freedom to stand and draw can be exploited by a card-counting player in chemin de fer, where it could not in Punto Banco. For example, when no cards of value 5 through 8 remain in the deck, the player should always draw. Certain compositions of cards make departures from the above banker strategy advisable. A player holding the bank could therefore use a card-counting system not only to decide when to raise his bet, but also to make correct playing decisions. It's therefore possible that a skilled player could gain a long-run advantage through card-counting. Downton and Lockwood unfortunately admit that the task of devising accurate banker playing strategies for different compositions of cards was beyond them. However, anyone who could succeed in devising such a positive expectation for the banker might well become very wealthy indeed. Unfortunately, the restrictions generally placed on the banker in the game as it is played today may well prevent this.

Downton and Lockwood do advise a simple card-counting strategy, which, incidentally, they say can also be used for other forms of baccarat. They advise keeping a mental count of the ratio of 10s to other cards, and 5s through 8s to other cards. Their betting strategy is to bet as a player when the 10s-to-others ratio is greater than two and the ratio of 5s through 8s to others is less than 0.5. In this situation, the player should always draw on 5. He should accept the bank when the 10s ratio is less than two and the 5 to 8s ratio is greater than 0.5. Otherwise the player should not bet.

Such a strategy will limit the player's losses and ensure a reasonable degree of participation, but it is not a winning strategy, and may be regarded as requiring too much mental effort for the casual player.

Tell-Play

"Tells" are known as giveaway signals of body language which indicate the value of a player's concealed cards. Tell-play is an outgrowth of the science of kinesics. If a player can read the body language of his opponents with even a small degree of accuracy he will gain a useful advantage. Tell-play is a science which was pioneered by players of poker, where it has proved very effective. It has also been recently used with devastating effect at the blackjack tables. The two classics on this science are Mike Caro's *Book of Tells—The Body Language of Poker* and Steve Forte's work on blackjack, *Read the Dealer*. While no publication specifically on tell-play in chemin de fer exists, the methods described in these works are easily applicable and translatable to this game. Tells are particularly useful against amateur players. A tell does not have to be accurate 100 percent of the time to be of value, just more often than not.

Typical tells are lip-sucking and biting, pupil dilation, and an overly confident posture, indicating the player holds a favorable hand. A hand over the mouth indicates an attempt to deceive. Folded arms are a defensive gesture, suggesting the player is "protecting" a poor total.

Table Betting Ranges

Typical table minimums are usually around $20. This may be much higher in more prestigious casinos. Table maximums can go up to $200,000, and sometimes there is no limit at all, since the casino is running none of the risk.

8

Baccarat en Banque

Baccarat en Banque, also known as *baccarat à deux tableaux* (two-table baccarat), is the oldest form of baccarat. It is actually played on one table whose layout is divided into two halves. A variety of it is known as *baccarat à tout va,* meaning "anything goes" or "no limits." This version is a game without restriction on betting stakes. It is not for the faint-hearted. It is not uncommon for players to win or lose the equivalent of $1 million in a single session.

In this version of baccarat, the punters are not allowed to be, or to bet on, the banker. This position is held permanently by an employee of the house, or by a syndicate which shares its profits with the house. Each punter takes a seat with a numbered position on it. Gamblers may bet either on player one or player two by placing their wagers on the appropriate marked spot. They may also bet on both (half their stake on each) by placing their wagers on the line between the two strips. The banker deals all the cards himself. He will deal three hands—initially two cards each to player one and then player two. This is the first player on the banker's right and the first player on the banker's left. Then he deals two cards to himself.

These cards are dealt face down. If the banker or either player has a natural, it is immediately declared and the hand is settled. If one player has a natural 8 or 9, but the other player and the banker do not, the game proceeds in the usual way for the player without the natural and the banker.

Player one draws a third card first, if the drawing-and-standing rules given in Chapter 1 require it. Again, he has the option to draw or stand on a total of 5. Then player two draws or stands in the same manner. The banker then decides whether to draw or stand, and has complete freedom in doing this. All third cards are dealt face-up. The highest hand wins and bets are settled. If both acting players win, then the payoff is 1 to 1. If both players lose, then both player bets are lost. If one hand wins and the other loses, or if both hands tie, then no money changes hands. If one of the two hands ties, the player wins half his bet if the other hand wins, or loses half his bet if the other hand loses. Players remain "active" if they win, otherwise the deal moves on to the next highest numbered player on the layout.

The players should lose at the rate of 0.92 percent per hand, assuming they and the banker play the best strategies. This rarely happens, of course, and the banker is usually more skilled than the players, so this figure is likely to be higher in actual play. Note that because the house banks the game, no commission is charged to the banker. The casino takes its profit from the banker's 1 percent edge, plus any advantage it may gain from skillful play on the part of the banker.

Winning Strategies

Baccarat en banque may be one of a few games where it is possible to win consistently. This is because the banker's strategy is usually directed towards the side of the table which wagers the most money. Consequently, the best strategy is often to bet on the side of the table which is wagering the least amount of money. The bank will then be playing a less than perfect strategy against your favored hand.

It is better to bet on player two than player one, because player two has the advantage of seeing player one's third card, if one is drawn. If the two players are wagering the same amount of money, the correct strategy on a total of 5 is similar to that used in chemin de fer: draw 82 percent of the time. There are complicated alterations to this strategy when the wagers are uneven, however.

Downton and Lockwood presented a complicated table of best strategies in their article "Computer Studies of Baccarat II: Baccarat-banque" (*Journal of the Royal Statistical Association*, 1976), based on different amounts of money wagered. They are not reproduced here, because of their complexity and because a gambler is not in control of the amounts wagered by both sides of the table, and only occasionally will have control of the option to draw or stand on 5.

Nevertheless, Downton and Lockwood prove that both player one and player two can, in certain circumstances, have a positive expected gain.

Player's Drawing Frequency on 5 When Player One is Dealt

Division of Natural Stakes	0	1	2	3	4	5	6	7	8	9	No Card	
0	.82	.82	.82	.82	.82	.82	.82	.82	.82	.82	.82	.82
0.1	.91	.91	.91	.82	.82	.82	.82	.82	.82	.82	.82	.82
0.2	.82	1	1	1	1	.91	.82	.82	.82	.91	.82	.82
0.3	1	1	1	1	1	.91	.91	.82	.91	1	.91	.82
0.4	.82	1	1	.82	1	.82	.82	.82	.91	.91	.82	.82
0.5	0	1	1	1	1	1	.82	.82	1	.91	.82	.82
0.6	1	.49	.82	1	1	.91	.82	.82	1	.49	.82	.82
0.7	1	1	.49	1	1	1	.82	.82	1	1	.82	.82
0.8	1	1	1	0	1	1	.82	.35	.82	0	.82	.82

Downton and Lockwood calculated that with an imbalance of 1 to 10, the player wagering the lesser amount had a very slight positive expected gain; this assumes that the two players and the banker are all playing their best strategies.

These factors make it difficult to say whether you could gain a practical edge at the game. My suggested strategy for the casual player would be this:

1. Bet on player two when only one-third or less of the total money wagered is on this side of the table.
2. Follow the above drawing strategy when you become the active player.
3. Use the counting system described by Downton and Lockwood for chemin de fer to determine when and when not to play.

My tentative conclusion is that the player should then be able to play with a small profit, but I am tentative because:

1. The player's edge will depend on the ability of the banker (see below).
2. The player rarely gets to be the active player.
3. The effects of card-counting in *baccarat en banque* have not yet been investigated (the effects of removal may differ from what happens in chemin de fer, though probably not significantly.
4. A proper winning approach would require every player to make decisions on behalf of player two to follow the correct strategy. In fact, players rarely know the correct strategy. The only solution to this would be for a team of skilled gamblers to monopolize all the seats on player two's side of the table.

Finally, could the two sides of the table conspire together to follow a strategy to beat the banker? This is expressly forbidden by the rules of the game, but would be impossible to prevent in practice. Unfortunately, the answer appears to be that it would not succeed. If the players do combine their strategies in order to beat the banker, the lowest to which they can reduce his edge is 0.85 percent, again assuming that all three protagonists play perfectly.

The Skill of the Banker

While the players may be able to gain from exercising card-counting strategies in *baccarat en banque*, there is some evidence that the banker can also. Some, particularly syndicate bankers, are reported to have excellent card memorization skills and mathematical knowledge. They are also supposedly skilled in deducing the strength of opponents' hands by their mannerisms. A banker with such abilities is probably playing at a greater advantage than the average 0.92 percent he would enjoy simply by playing the best strategy without employing any knowledge of the unused cards. I would therefore not advise playing against a banker who appears to study the cards intently or displays an unusual interest in an active player's body language. By contrast, some house bankers seem to display an ignorance of the correct drawing-and-standing decisions. It is possible to estimate an approximate 1 percent edge they would enjoy by using correct strategy.

Although *baccarat en banque* is not the most popular form of the game, it is probably the form most representative of its image. The sums bet are greater than at any other form of gambling on earth, with the possible exception of the stock market. Considering the potential rewards, it is perhaps surprising that winning strategies have not been investigated more closely.

Yin Yang Yo

For years pit bosses at casinos and gaming clubs around the world have dreamed of combining the popular appeal and excitement of blackjack with the diverse wagering of baccarat. Many blackjack-baccarat mutations have been devised over the years, but most have deservedly been forgotten, although a game has recently been introduced in certain casinos in Las Vegas and Atlantic City which really does capture the best elements of both games. At the present time, the rules of this new game have not been fully standardized, but its main structure (taken from a casino flyer) is given below:

Yin Yang "Yo-22"
(Patent no. 5,072,946)
There are four different bets—Yin, Yang, Yo, or the Flaming Flamingo.
Bet on which hand will come closest to 22, or if they will tie.
There are two opposing hands dealt, Yin and Yang, each receiving one card. The hand with the lowest value receives the next card until there is a Yo (a tie), or the Yin (silver) or Yang (gold) busts [goes over 22].

That's all there is to it.

Yin wins if the Yang hand goes over 22.

Yang wins if the Yin hand goes over 22.

[Yo wins 2–9 natural on the come-out or any other tie under 22.]

[Yo wins A–7 natural on the come-out or any other tie under 22.]

[The "come out" is defined as the first two cards dealt, one to each hand.]

Side bet: Flaming Flamingo—both hands tie on 22.

[On a 22 tie, Yo loses, Yin and Yang push.]

[On a 22 tie, Yin, Yang and Yo push.]

Nonmatching face cards (K-Q, K-J, Q-J) on the come-out—all bets lose

[All other ties (10–A) on the come-out continue counting.]

[All other ties (8–K) on the come-out continue counting.]

Yin, Yang, and Yo pay 2–1 each. Side bet pays 55–1.

Wager on any bet or combinations.

[Double payouts with two or more Bonus Jokers on winning bet.]

[Double, triple, or quadruple payouts with two, three, or four bonus Jokers on winning bet.]

[Everyone wins double on a Flaming Flamingo with two Bonus Jokers.]

[Everyone wins double, triple, or quadruple on a Flaming Pearl with two, three, or four Bonus Jokers.]

[Main bet, $2–$200. Side bet, $1–$25]

This game has been increasingly popular since some casinos have adopted it. It is the first new game devised where players will actually desert the standard casino table games. Evidently its popular appeal has much to do with the not-overwhelming house edge, but it appears to make a great deal for the house also, as the pace of the game is extremely fast, which allows the casinos to take in faster action per hour. Its introduction to the American Indian and Riverboat casinos and the casinos of Great Britain is anticipated shortly.

9

Super Pan Nine

The deregulation of gambling in California led to the invention of a new and interesting game known as Super Pan Nine. While the game is a recent innovation, it harkens back to the spirit of the older baccarat games. Syndicates have formed in California to challenge the game, depending on their card skill for their advantage, much as the European syndicates formed to take on all-comers with *baccarat en banque.*

The game has two versions, one in which the bank can be held by the players, and one in which the casino is the permanent banker. The game uses six or eight decks stripped of 7s, 8s, 9s, and 10s (face cards are not removed). The players and banker are dealt three cards face down. The players decide whether to draw a fourth card or not, with the object of getting a total as close to 9 as possible. They have complete discretion on whether to draw the fourth card.

Scoring is the same as in other forms of baccarat. If a fourth card is drawn, this will be dealt face up. If the casino is banking the game, the house will draw a fourth card if its total is between 0 and 5, but not otherwise. If a player holds the bank, he has the freedom to draw as he wishes. The higher total wins and no money changes hands in the event of a tie. There is a side bet on a tie with a 7 to 1 payoff. Players and player-bankers are each paid off at 19 to 20 if they win.

The player-banker has the advantage of seeing the player's fourth card (if there is any). No thorough analysis of the game exists, but it is known that a banker playing against a single opponent can have a 1 percent edge. As in *baccarat en banque,* the banker's strategy will be aimed at the player who wagers the most money, meaning a player wagering a relatively low amount can sometimes play with a positive expectation if he adjusts his playing strategy accordingly. If you wish to investigate the game further, read Mason Malmuth's *Gambling Theory and Other Topics.*

No work has currently been done on the potential of card-counting at Super Pan Nine, but the freedom to draw and stand on the third card would suggest that it may be worthy of investigation, owing to the greater importance of skilled play. Intuitively, it seems that the player could gain some advantage by keeping a ratio of cards Ace, 2, and 3, to 4, 5, and 6, for the purposes of determining whether to stand on 5 or 6, which are marginal decisions with a full pack.

This game has recently been introduced to a few American casinos outside California on an experimental basis. It has been successfully introduced to the larger casinos of Britain.

10

Tournament Baccarat

A development of interest to baccarat players has been the emergence of the tournament. This offers gamblers the chance to play against each other, rather than the house. In theory, this means a skilled player could consistently win money.

Typically players "buy in" the tournament for a certain amount of money. They are usually given nonnegotiable "fantasy chips" in return, or they must sometimes take that amount of their own cash into the game. In either case, every tournament entrant will have exactly the same amount to begin with. Then the entrants will play baccarat in small groups, against the dealer, using all the rules as in ordinary baccarat. Players take turns in betting first, as the knowledge of how other players have bet is useful information. The object is to have the most cash at the end of the "round"—a fixed amount of time or number of hands. The winners compete on through successive rounds in a process of gradual elimination until an overall victor has been established.

Before entering a tournament, it is always advisable to find out how much of the players' buy-in fees are returned in the form of prizes. In some cases, this may be 100 percent. Obviously, for the player seeking to make money, the higher percentage, the better. For a tournament, a player's strategy must be very different from what it would be in a normal game. Generally, the tournament will not last very long, probably not to the end of the shoe. This rules out strategies such as card-counting, which will have virtually no effect in the short term. A good strategy is to bet big until you gain the lead, and then small as your opponents try to catch up. To get into the lead, it is often necessary to bet on the tie. As we have seen, the tie is a much less favorable bet than the bank or the player, but because of the 9 to 1 payoff, if you should hit on a lucky sequence of ties and are betting heavily, you will be very difficult to catch. Syndicates of tie bettors have been known to walk out of tourneys with the big prizes on a regular basis. At the beginning of the game, you want to "maximize variance," i.e., give yourself the best chance of a big win even at the expense of a greater chance of losing heavily, since there is no prize for second place.

If you gain the lead, you really want to "minimize variance" to stay in front, so you should bet small and preferably on banker. One killer strategy is to put a "lock" on your opponents. This involves mirroring the bets of your opponents, so if you are in the lead and the player who has the next highest amount of chips to you bets $50 on the player, then you do exactly the same. This way, it's impossible for him to gain the lead, since what's good for him is good for you. In the final round, the strategy is simple: bet everything you can in order to win, which may or may not necessitate betting on the tie. If you don't have to do this, bet on the banker, as it has a greater than 50 percent chance of winning. If you are in the lead, beware of players betting the tie, as a single spectacular coup at the end often puts a lowly-placed player into the lead.

Teams can be used to good effect in tournaments. Although the mathematically expected return can be quite high for a skilled tournament player (often well over 50 percent), making a living from tourneys is not practical because to actually make any money requires winning the contest (or coming in second or third in larger casinos), which is a rare compensation for the vast majority of times you will finish nowhere. This means you would need a huge bankroll to last out these long losing periods.

Teams can solve this problem. A team's collective chance of having a member win the tournament is obviously higher than an individual's, and profits will be split among team members. They effectively get into the final run faster and reduce the fluctuations in their capital.

One strategy used by early team players was simple but highly effective. Two players would sit at the same table and bet the minimum on the banker or player. They would do this until the last hand, when one would bet the table maximum on bank, while the other would bet the table maximum on winning the round. Note the similarity between this technique and the strategy of maximum boldness. This strategy is extremely effective against ordinary players who are generally far too conservative, but it may be less effective with the growth in the sophistication of tournament players.

If you are going to enter a tournament, it is a good idea to practice eyeballing stacks of chips to determine their total value. Knowing exactly how many chips each player has is a very important and valuable skill, and essential to a winning approach. Generally speaking, a stack of ten chips measures about one-and-a-quarter inches.

Your strategy should be to avoid making large bets until the last few hands, thus preserving your bankroll. Your large bets will give you a much greater chance of winning if they are made with the knowledge of your opponents' wins and losses, and what you can make of their strategy. If you have wasted your bankroll early on, you will miss the opportunity to use the information about your opponents that you have learned. Note the similarity between this strategy and the strategy of long-distance runners, who pace themselves for the early part of a race and then break into a sprint, using up their remaining energy when the finishing line is in sight.

Tournament baccarat is also a little like poker. The player who uses a predictable strategy will have his actions anticipated by his opponents and will end up at a serious disadvantage. Remember, also, that sometimes all the players will be wiped out by a bad streak, and merely by having one chip left at the end of the round you might win. The best betting decision, both on what to wager and how much, is often not obvious.

Tournaments are very exciting, even if played for comparatively low stakes, since pride as well as money is at stake. At the larger tourneys, the turn of a friendly card can make the difference between winning or losing tens of thousands of dollars. Despite the competition, tourneys generate a friendly atmosphere of celebration; they also provide a rare opportunity to show off your knowledge of gambling. Many players enjoy tourneys so much they make them the highlight of their trip.

For those players seeking to make serious money from baccarat tournament play, I suggest reading Stanford Wong's *Casino Tournament Strategy*. Wong states that very big money can be won by skilled players in the baccarat tourneys periodically offered on the West Coast of the United States. There is more money to be made at baccarat tourneys than almost any other form of gambling, and skill is of importance, though a great deal of luck is required to win. At the highest level, admission to baccarat tourneys is by invitation only, and very expensive.

11

Playing for Comps

A "comp" (complimentary) is a freebie or price reduction given to you by the casino to encourage you to stay and gamble. It may take a number of forms—it could be free breakfast, a show, a room, a meal at the restaurant. It usually takes the form of a chit or token that you hand to the waitress, hostess, or waiter. The comp effectively states that the casino will pay for the service you require. Nevada alone gives away $500 million worth of complimentaries every year.

A comp is only given out for a single purpose, that is, the casino knows it will encourage you to lose more at their tables than you would otherwise. Many gamblers feel that by getting comps they are getting something for nothing, consequently, they gamble recklessly since they believe they are already ahead, and lose more overall (including the price of the comp) than they would otherwise.

To get a comp, you must ask. Comps are never given retroactively; they are an inducement to further gambling, so the casino has no interest in comping you as you leave. Anyone can get a comp, regardless of their bet size, although the value of the comp will, of course, vary.

First you must get "rated." Tell the pit boss you want to be rated. You will need to show him some ID. He will assess your buy-in (the amount of chips you bought to begin gambling with) or typical bet size to determine whether you are eligible. A floor man will then keep track of your buy-in, your initial bet, and your win-loss ratio. This data will be processed in a computer at the end of the day.

Many casinos (particularly those in Atlantic City) will tell you that they cannot rate you for a typical bet of less than $10 to $25. If this is the case, do not up the size of your bet. It is not worth losing twice as much in order to gain some small freebie. If you do not get rated, you may be eligible for a comp in any case if you are persistent and assertive. You must ask the casino host or the floor man in the pit where you are playing for an appropriate comp, whatever you want and think your betting justifies. It is good psychology to maintain eye contact as you do this, as it is more persuasive.

There will be a casino host specifically dealing with table games or baccarat. It is important you strike up a good relationship with these individuals, because it is their job to see that you have fun and come back. Be polite and friendly. Refer to them by their first name, and ask for them when you make a reservation.

By cultivating contacts you will be able to shop around for the best deals. Before a trip, call various casinos you know and ask them what you're worth in comp value (they probably have you on computer). Haggle, and then take the best deal. Some talented individuals can twist the comp game to their advantage, so they lose less at the tables than they make in comps. Max Rubin's *Comp City* is the best book on this subject. Rubin states that a skilled comp hustler could get back $1 for every 20 cents in losses. Of course, professional gamblers do not play for comps, they play for money, but everyone should attempt to maximize their comp value.

Baccarat is in many ways the natural game for the comp hustler. Its small house edge and the large average bet make it a natural choice. Most of the luxuries the casino pays for will go to baccarat high rollers.

As a general rule, your comp will be worth 30 percent of your average bet in an hour. For the ordinary gambler who is not using a winning technique, he will be losing 1.06 percent on every hand, assuming he always bets on the bank, which he should. This is not only because he will lose less than on other wagers; it is also because the cumbersome 19 to 20 payoff slows down the game considerably, and the slower the game, the fewer the hands, and the fewer the hands, the less you will lose. You can try betting amounts which are difficult to work out the commission for, and then vary these bets so the croupier must perform different arithmetic with every bet, which will slow the game down even further.

Periodically leave the table to smoke, visit the lavatory, or take a drink. Provided you do not leave for too long, the floor man will not subtract the time spent not betting from your comp value.

You can further slow down the croupier by asking about the rules of the game as it is in progress. There is nothing unusual in this; few players fully understand the drawing-and-standing rules. If the floor man is displaying interest in your game, raise your bet, then lower it when his attention is elsewhere. Peripheral vision can be very useful here. With casino personnel who are not wise to these tricks, you can substantially cut your expenses and may even make a small profit.

It's a good idea for the player trying to get comps to use a simple card-counting method, such as the one described in Chapter 3, to minimize losses. Casino personnel don't know anything about counting at baccarat and will assume you're losing at the same rate as any other player. Saving $120 on every $1,000 bet isn't a fantastic savings but it may well make the difference between making a profit or an overall loss on comps.

For players using the advantage-play techniques described earlier, you can still get comps, but most of the time your average bet size will be the table minimum, so don't expect the five-star suite. Moreover, it is not in your interest to slow the game down, as you have the advantage and it would lead to you making less money. You may also feel, however, that being rated is attention you do not want from casino personnel, who may become suspicious if you win consistently.

While it's certainly possible to beat the system, comp enthusiasts often forget that comps aren't equivalent to their monetary value, because the casino decides what you can do with the money. There will come a point at which you run out of hard cash. Because of this, it's not possible to make a living from comps, though the intelligent player, with a little trickery, may get himself a luxurious all-expenses paid holiday.

Junkets

A gambling "junket" is a free trip offered by a casino to an organization. It is simply another part of the corporate hospitality business. It will usually be to a gambling city, such as Atlantic City or Las Vegas, though junkets may also take clients to places such as London or Puerto Rico, where gambling is legalized. There is usually a deal between the casino and the organization; often they will be offspring of a parent company.

The casino pays for the players' travel, hotel, and other expenses. In return, the clients put up a sum of money, say $1,000. When they reach the casino this will be returned in the form of special nonnegotiable chips, i.e., they can only be used to gamble in one particular casino and their value cannot be redeemed. They will also be distinctively marked so they cannot be mistaken for other chips. In theory, this is a good deal for both sides. The clients get a free trip and the casino gets a set of highly-paid executives at their tables, most of whom probably don't know the first thing about gambling and don't know when to quit.

Qualification for a junket doesn't come easy. The player's credentials must already be well established by the tour operator, or you must be referred by someone who is both trusted and whose reputation is valued highly.

The downside of junkets for the players is that they are monitored both by the junket operator and by casino officials. Often they will use computers to verify exactly how much and how long you bet. This harassment can seriously compromise your vacation. If you don't come up to scratch they may cancel your travel reimbursement and your complimentaries. Requirements for play vary, depending on the costs involved in the junket, but minimum bets generally must be high. Typically, the casino might want to stipulate that you play four hours of baccarat a day, putting up $100 bets.

How should you play when you go on a junket? Well, it depends on what you're trying to achieve. If you're trying to give yourself the best chance of a big win, put it all on the bank and hope. This is very risky, though. If you lose, you either have to start digging into your own money to bet or leave the tables, which will almost certainly cause difficulties with the junket operator.

Ideally, you want the most risk-free way of getting your money back. A good way of doing this is to get a friend to bet his chips on the player while you bet on the banker. If the player wins, you have reclaimed a chip's worth of money, and the hand pushes. If the bank wins, you lose 5 percent of the chips value, which is not an excessive amount. Slowly, you will get back all of your investment in usable chips (which can be turned into hard cash) without risking going broke in the process. It's best to make this process as protracted as possible in order to spend enough time at the tables so as not to make the casino too suspicious. Then you will be able to enjoy the rest of the vacation. *Never* start dipping into your own money—that's when you start to lose out on the deal.

12

The Internet

Recently, there has been much interest in the opening of several on-line "casinos," virtual gaming parlors you can visit without leaving your home and which exist only in cyberspace on your computer screen. For a long time, there have been computer programs created for you to play your favorite casino games, including baccarat, but the difference is that you can now play for real money via the Internet.

To join an Internet casino requires you to have computer access and to provide the casino you wish to join with your credit card details. It is for this reason that many people are very suspicious of these organizations. Every time you play a game, your account is debited or credited automatically with the amount that you win or lose.

Naturally, baccarat is not the first choice for an Internet casino. Sixty percent of the pleasure of playing baccarat is in the ambience the game creates. Obviously, this does not translate too well to a computer screen. It is ridiculous to imagine a tuxedoed high roller obtaining the same pleasure from a computer game with badly animated graphics and irritating blipping noises as he would from the casino game proper. Nevertheless, some casinos do offer the game. Personally, I feel this is a desecration of the spirit of baccarat.

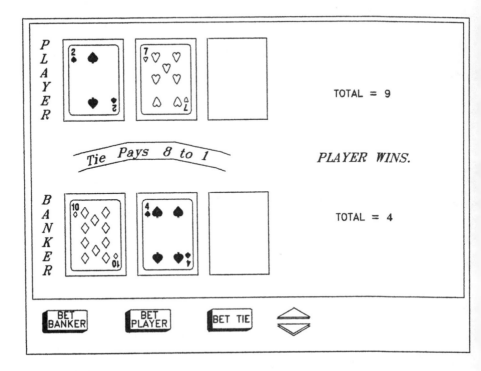

A typical screen layout of an Internet baccarat game

The rules are typically identical to that of ordinary baccarat. As with most long-distance computer communication, the games are slow and jerky, and considering the level of sophistication that computer graphics have achieved in the last few years of the twentieth century, the presentation at the time of writing (1998) is still surprisingly poor. The table maximums and minimums are much lower than they would be in regular baccarat. This is because the casinos fear that they could lose large sums of money to hackers.

The cards are "shuffled" much more thoroughly than in any human shuffle. This is because the cards are dealt according to a pseudo-random number. This is a series of numbers that appear completely unconnected with each other but do, in fact, follow a very complex series. If you could figure this series out you could predict what cards would be dealt and make a lot of money. Unfortunately, this is very difficult to do. You will not find how to do this in any library; it is a very important part of military intelligence (it is connected with code-breaking) and writings on the subject are usually kept confidential.

I do not recommend that you have anything to do with baccarat on the Internet. This is simply because it is far too easy for the casino to cheat, or to put it more politely, "bias" the system against the punter. A program can easily be written to appear to offer a fair game of baccarat, yet actually favor the house so the player loses far more per hand than in the casino game. If you are cheated, there is no way to prove it and nothing you could do about it, even if it could be proven. The casinos are often based in some banana republic military dictatorship with little legislation or interest in prosecuting some obscure case on a foreigner's behalf.

If you are still interested, I can only offer the following advice:

1. Only join an Internet casino that claims to offer baccarat with the same odds as the real casino game, and preferably one which has been independently tested for accuracy. This is by no means a guarantee that the game is honest, but without such an assurance the game is almost certainly dishonest.

2. Most cyberspace casinos will have software that you can download and play without actually having to risk money. Play a few hundred hands of baccarat and see if this accords with your experience in the real world. Any serious fixing of the game would probably become apparent. Again, the software you can download and play for free is not necessarily the same as the software you use when playing for actual money, but if the free software does not accord with your experience of actual baccarat you can bet your life the play-for-money software is rigged too.

3. If you sign on to a casino and play for real stakes, then keep a careful tally of your wins and losses and the number of hands you have played. If you are unsure whether you are being cheated, take out a statistics textbook and do a chi-squared or Poisson

distribution test on your results, which will give you a good indication. If the idea of setting out to do this fills you with mathematical dread, then you could try posting a question to one of the mathematics or gambling news groups on the Internet, and you will probably find that there is someone who is willing and able to perform these calculations for you.

4. Never join an Internet casino which states in its rules something to the effect that "For personal rather than professional use only." This usually means, "No journalists or other individuals who might expose us for the crooks we are—strictly suckers only." If it has nothing to hide, it would not fear investigation. The reputable casinos will invite independent testers to try out their software in order to verify its fairness.

5. Only buy in to any such organization for the absolute minimum, at least until you've established you're getting a fair deal.

6. Try to find out other people's experiences with the casino before you join. If you look in the archives at http://www.dejanews.com, you may find many uncensored stories about people's dealings with many of the operational casinos.

7. Do *not* tolerate any delay in payment of winnings you have rightfully won. Do *not* listen to any excuses or put up with any procrastination. There is no reasonable excuse. What's more likely, they are trying to withhold payment for as long as possible in order to accumulate interest on money which has been won legitimately by their clients, if, indeed, they have any intention of paying you at all.

13

Pyschology

The most important questions you should ask yourself before playing baccarat for the first time are: What type of person am I? and What do I expect from the game?

Apart from "professionals" and cheaters, who are not part of the broad mass of ordinary players, there are mainly two types of player who enter a baccarat game. First, there is the type the casinos would have us believe comprises the only group they are interested in serving—the casual player. He considers himself simply to be taking in a little entertainment, and looks on the money he loses to the house as a fair price to pay for the thrill of gambling, the surrounding finery, and the respect and subservience accorded to him by casino personnel. He occasionally bets big, but plays only for a few hours or so in a week; the casino is merely a part of his social movements. Usually he will not be alone, and he may bring a girlfriend along.

The second type is all too familiar to us: the compulsive gambler. His entire life revolves around the painful extraction of his money in the hours he gets to spend in the casino. He has little or no understanding of probability, and chains himself to the table. He may follow some system, probably similar in character to those mentioned in Chapter 2. He may well have had an initial period of success with his system.

Gradually and slowly, he loses his winnings and falls significantly behind. He takes his losses personally; he associates them with personal failings and feelings of inadequacy. He recognizes patterns in the cards where none exist and blindly attempts to follow them. He tries to follow streaks, like most of the literature on baccarat informs him to do. He may blame his failure to beat the house on "bad luck" or "lack of discipline."

The compulsive gambler comes from all walks of life; he is not more likely to be poor or badly educated. Some compulsive gamblers may be very successful in their own field, since they have to be clever enough to have money in the first place, and then dumb enough to lose it—a weird paradox. They are, however, very unlikely to have any sort of mathematical background. Compulsive gamblers who play baccarat are particularly likely to be system players.

The traditional psychoanalyst's explanation for the behavior of compulsive gamblers is that they are motivated by deep personal self-loathing, probably due to some incident in their childhood. They are lured to the gaming tables by the promise of riches, but, subconsciously, they want to punish themselves by losing. Some cases certainly fit this profile, but more modern psychoanalytical thought recognizes the complexity of the lure of gambling. The simple guilt theory is by no means accurate in all cases. Many gamblers genuinely believe they can beat the house. Some are attracted to the comforting womblike atmosphere of the baccarat pit. Almost all gamblers are addicted to the heightened flow of adrenaline induced by the risk of playing for high stakes. To blame all compulsive gambling behavior on some masochistic desire is an unhelpful and unnecessary generalization.

To avoid ever developing a gambling habit, it's a good idea to develop a few personal rules. First, always take a watch to a casino. Because they don't have clocks, it's easy to play for far longer and bet substantially more than you might have originally intended. NEVER leave yourself any access to other funds; take the amount of money to the casino that you can afford to lose and no more. Never take a credit card with you. Never "steam," i.e., bet bigger and bigger on a losing streak in an attempt to recoup your losses—this is a sure route to disaster.

Always keep a picture of the true worth of the amounts you're betting, as it's very easy to switch yourself off and no longer make any connection between gambling chips and actual value. If you are winning, put aside what you came with and bet from your winnings only. Many writers call this "playing with their money." Of course, you're not doing this at all; as soon as you won it became yours, but this strategy significantly increases your chances of staying ahead of the casino in a single session.

If you came by train or bus, make sure you have a return ticket to get home. Never have any illusions about casino personnel. By all means be cordial, but remember that they are interested in only one thing: removing as much money from you as quickly and painlessly as possible.

Never drink alcohol! This is one of the most potent weapons casinos possess; they do not ply you with free drinks out of generosity. Always remember to keep track of the amount of commissions owed on winning bank hands. It would be very embarrassing to have to leave the game and find you could not pay off the amount you owe, and might well result in your being barred from the casino.

A word about attitude. Remember, all gamblers will experience wild streaks of fortune, both good and bad. At big-table baccarat, it's unacceptable to swear and display overt emotion when losing. This might come as news to players of other table games who wish to "graduate" to the prestige game, but such behavior shows you as a novice. The seasoned players know that taking their losses in stride is part of the overhead, and you will gain respect for keeping a casual demeanor when every card seems to turn against you. By the same token, do not rub your success in other players' faces. A man of genuine character has enough class never to make other people feel second rate. Remember that all gambling, and baccarat in particular, has its fair share of highs and lows. Don't feel persecuted by a series of losing sessions. Watch the cool demeanor of the high-rolling Asians who play the game. This is one area of life where we can learn from the East. In Western society we are taught always to strive for success, which is won only through strength of character. We are told there is a macho personality who can bend lady luck to his will. In Eastern society, there is an entirely different attitude towards fate that better understands what can and cannot be changed.

Never forget that everything the casino does is done in order to make money. This includes the inducements it offers to encourage further play. Coupons, comps, promotions, and junkets are offered for one reason and one reason only: to encourage players to drop more at the tables than they would otherwise. They know that the average player on a junket and the lavishly comp'ed high roller will consider themselves several thousand dollars ahead before they get to the tables. Because of this, they will bet more recklessly than they would otherwise. If they begin to lose they will remain betting at higher levels, for, after all, they have "wasted" their advantage over the casino and know that they now have to get it back. If they are winning, they will disregard any initial caution they might have had about betting big. They are invincible. After all, if they weren't men of wealth and status, why would the casino treat them in the first place? Therefore, ruin, or at least a painful loss, becomes inevitable. Because of complimentaries, a high roller may end up losing several hundred thousand more than he would have had he not received them.

The casinos use psychology in far more subtle ways and have a number of techniques to relieve you of your cash without your realizing it. Chips look like colored coins—this is not accidental. Coins are thought of as having inconsequential value. Players are encouraged to make a subconscious association with coins, as this will cause them to spend more recklessly. Baccarat gaming chips are invariably larger than other chips. There is no reason for this except to enhance the atmosphere of the high-rolling mystique that the game evokes.

You will rarely find a clock or windows in a casino. A clock or the rising of the dawn would alert players to the length of time they have spent gambling. This would shake them from the trancelike state induced by the intense fascination of the ritual of baccarat. It's very easy to lose track of time in this manner. At times, it's like being at a religious ceremony. The plush womblike atmosphere of the classier casinos (where baccarat is usually offered) has a comforting effect on players.

It's an unreal world, and leaving the casino is sometimes like a harsh awakening from a dream.

A coupon is much less of an inducement to play than a comp suite, but it works similar trickery on the low-rollers' mind. He may not have planned to go out gambling that night, but since the casino people offered that free coupon, why not take them up on it? After all, it's the casino's money. Except, of course, that once you're sitting at the table it's almost impossible to get up again. If you win, then you're still only playing with the casino's money, aren't you? If you lose, well, all you have to do is double the bet to come up ahead again, right?

Note how gamblers have a justification for all kinds of irrational behavior. It doesn't really have anything to do with self-control or determination; many compulsive gamblers are successful people who have displayed talent and dedication to get on in their respective careers. It's just a part of human nature.

Always resist the temptation to get involved in personal conflicts at the table. Quite often I've seen players take an irrational dislike to each other at the table over some imagined slight, and then get into a war by placing bets on the banker, while the other does so on player, each one trying to psyche the other out. This can lead to players betting beyond their means. In this situation, no one wins except the house. Leave your ego at home; there is no place for it on the felt. If you take a dislike to somebody who plays at your table, or they take a dislike to you—then leave. If you're not enjoying the game, there is no point in staying.

The attitude of regular gamblers is that fellow players should be seen neither as friends nor strangers but as colleagues. You all have a common interest, but the intensity of involvement in the gambling process means that regular socializing is awkward and distracting. Nevertheless, many friendships are formed at the table.

Friends you take into the casino from the outside world are another matter. I recommend you do this as often as possible, because knowing when to quit and doing it are two different things. A good way to force yourself to quit is to take a friend or partner along, set a stop-loss limit, and tell him or her that it's cashing-in time. Your friend won't be as wrapped-up in gambling as you will be, and will be able to see reason to quit when you no longer can.

At the highest levels of play, the baccarat player learns as much about himself as he does about the game. Gamblers often find that their true nature emerges as they play. If you see faults in your character appearing as you play—impatience, arrogance, anger—try to recognize and correct them. Be gracious in your success and philosophical in your losses. You may not always beat the house, but you will become a grand master of that other game, life.

14

Baccarat Miscellanea

I promised you everything you ever wanted to know about baccarat and a good deal more besides. Here's the besides:

1. Playing cards are purchased by the casino in lots of 100,000 decks.
2. Baccarat layouts cost around $120. They are changed every two to three months, depending on use.
3. When the casino tells you the hotel is fully booked, it isn't. The best suites will be kept open for a handful of sheikhs, despotic leaders of various military juntas, and people who work for Microsoft. They are unlikely to turn up, but just in case they do, the casino is playing it safe. These individuals will lose more in a few nights at the baccarat table than a busload of slot players will in a lifetime.
4. The famous gambling scene in *Casino Royale*, when James Bond defeats his archenemy, the communist agent Le Chiffre, at the baccarat table is based on a real incident. In the days when Bond's creator, Ian Fleming, worked for MI6, the British secret service, he once stayed at the Palacio Hotel on the Tagus estuary in Estoril, which contained a plush casino. Fleming played against some local Portuguese businessmen for low stakes, and

lost in what was apparently a rather deflating evening. At the end of the session, Fleming remarked to a companion that if they had been playing against Russian agents the evening would have been more exciting, proving that fact is often duller than fiction.

5. Sean Connery, for many the archetypal Bond, actually knew nothing about the game he played with such confidence time and time again in the films. When a gambling author attempted to explain the rules to Connery in a casino, they were interrupted by an old lady asking for Connery's autograph. When she inquired what they were doing, Connery, anxious not to destroy the illusion, murmured that were discussing "advanced strategy." The old lady went away happy.

6. An Asian gentlemen by the name of Ken Mizuno rightly deserves the title of King of the High Rollers. This individual would think of nothing of betting $200,000 a hand for several days in a row. Over a two-year period in Las Vegas he ran up debts of $65 million, possibly the greatest amount of money a player has ever lost at baccarat, or any other gambling game.

7. John Aspinall, the proprietor of the semilegendary Aspinall's private club in London, made his fortune by introducing chemin de fer to the British, usually the British playboy. Despite the fact that he beggared many of his clients, he made a surprisingly good name for himself by never resorting to violence when attempting to reclaim gambling debts, which are not reclaimable in English law; he merely appealed to his customers' sense of honor and fair play. Only in England could you get this to work.

8. One elderly gentleman, on his seventieth birthday, was enjoying the pleasures of Las Vegas baccarat at the Tropicana. He bet a steady $200 and enjoyed a spectacularly unfavorable losing streak.

He bet every hand on the player. The pit remarked later that they had never seen so many endless banker streaks. The elderly gentlemen fell very, very far behind, losing $200,000 in only four or five hours worth of play. Before his capital was drained further, he remarked with calm assurance, "I think my luck will change now." He asked for the table maximum to be raised, and the casino manager agreed. Sticking grimly to the player despite the trend, the elderly gentlemen bet his remaining chips up to the new $200,001 limit and won, winning with a player total of 1 to the bank's 0. Taking his solitary dollar, he left with the words, "A winner knows when to quit." No one ever saw him again.

9. Chip collection is a hobby you might consider. Some might think it irrelevant, but it is, nonetheless, a useful and practical way to make money at baccarat. Keeping a chip as a souvenir of each casino visited is a common habit among gamblers, particularly the more superstitious players. Few of them probably realize that they may become valuable in years to come, and pay for many a losing session.

As with anything weird and useless, there is an army of obsessive individuals ready to buy up baccarat chips of historical value. These people spend their lives in search of the unusual curio, the final set in the series, reveling in the obscure background to each finding.

Of course, not every chip is of value; there has to be some special significance attached. These may be chips created specifically for a tournament or promotion, to commemorate an event of national importance, from abroad, or from several decades back. If you are going to retain a few chips from a baccarat session because you think their base value will be exceeded by their collectors value, it's best to do so when a few criteria are met.

As with all antiques, rarity can greatly enhance value. Complete sets of chips are naturally worth more than individual chips. They may often fetch fifteen to twenty times their base value, and because baccarat chips enjoy such pride of place in the chip hierarchy, and because their relatively high base value makes them a scarce commodity, even bigger profits can sometimes be realized. To find out more, try the *Collector's Guide to Nevada Gaming Checks and Chips,* Whitman Division, Western Publishing Co., 1220 Mound Ave., Racine, WI 53404.

If you hear that a casino is closing down, it is a good strategy to play there on its last night and hoard as many chips as you can risk taking. Their value will almost certainly increase with time.

10. Baccarat dealers enjoy a privileged position, earning up to $50,000 per year in the larger casinos. They typically receive significantly more on top of their basic pay in the form of tips. It's not unknown for a "whale" to leave a team of croupiers $10,000 or more after a single winning session.

15

The Future

Given the considerable evolution that baccarat has undergone during its long history, it would not be at all surprising if the character of the game were once again to alter fundamentally.

In the second edition of his book *How to Win at Casino Gambling*, Henry Tamburin describes an attempt at such an alteration. Recently, a number of casinos in Atlantic City and Las Vegas (most notably the Sahara and Sands) were experimenting with a form of baccarat in which the commission was removed from the bank bet. To compensate for this, the rules were slightly altered: a bank hand total of 4 and a player hand total from 0 to 3 was declared a tie. In another version, only half odds were paid on a winning banker total of 6.

The reason for this was simple. Baccarat profits have been steadily declining over the last few decades. The commission on the bank hand is known to be unpopular. Moreover, it slows down the pace of the game, and because fewer hands are dealt the casino's profits are reduced. Henry told me that this experiment was unsuccessful. This hardly seems surprising; players would tend to be cautious about a rule they did not understand and which appeared to have no simple logic to it.

I believe I have a better alternative: instead of charging a flat commission on the bank hand, which is effectively a tax and about as enjoyable as being taxed, the casino could declare a loss for the bank on all "natural" ties (i.e., on 8 or 9).

This would give the bank hand just about the same kind of house edge that it enjoys at the present time. The rule would be very similar to the *refait* in the French card game of *trente et quarante,* where it has proved to be a popular rule. The air of European sophistication about the game would be enhanced by the change, and it would add an element of fun for "hunch" gamblers who like to determine when an event is "due." Moreover, the casino could offer the player other options to increase interest in the game, such as an "insurance" wager against the probability of a tie at 8 or 9, or the *en prison* rule, used in roulette.

I believe this ought to be a much more attractive option to the punter, and it should increase the pace of the game greatly. Economically, this is very important for the casino, not only in terms of profits but also in the form of reduced risk. Baccarat revenue fluctuates dramatically because it depends on whether a handful of high rollers or the casino is luckiest in a given month. It is for this reason that Wall Street analysts do not consider baccarat when assessing economic trends on the Las Vegas Strip.

Baccarat is very serious business. In 1995, it was still making $595 million for the Las Vegas Strip, earning twice as much as blackjack per table, which is the much more popular game. Nevertheless, these impressive earnings will continue to decline year after year, creating even more volatility, unless remedial action is taken. The decline will be accelerated by the extent of the economic crisis in the Far East, which began at the end of 1997.

What possible relevance could that have for Las Vegas? Well, the majority of high rollers, defined typically as an individual who bets $10,000 a hand, come from Pacific Rim countries. Jack Binion, casino owner extraordinaire, estimated that 90 percent of his baccarat high rollers hailed from this region. At this time, it seems that these players may face dramatic reductions both in their numbers and in their disposable incomes as a result of the current Asian recession. Their problem will become a problem for Las Vegas, as well as for other areas which cater specifically to the high roller, such as London, unless the game is altered to become more populist, or a new type of high-stakes bettor emerges.

By removing the commission and doubling the amount of hands a high roller could play at the same time, the casinos would reduce their variance and stabilize their profits. Another idea to increase profits is this: when a tie occurs, instead of returning all money to player or bank bettors, decide the winner according to the value of the first card dealt by determining which is closest to 9. For example:

Player and bank both have three-card totals of 6. The banker received a 9 as his first card and the player received a 5, so in this instance the bank would win. This means that the 10 percent of all hands that are ties no longer represent a 0 percent investment for the house. The house edge remains static, but the casino's profits become greater.

If the first cards of the player and the bank hand are equal, then the values of the second cards in each hand should be determined. Also, no money changes hands in the unlikely event that these hands tie.

A final suggestion is to introduce the "surrender" rule popularized by Atlantic City blackjack and roulette. In baccarat, the surrender option would allow a player to surrender his bet after the first four cards have been dealt if he forfeits half his stake in exchange for the return of the rest of the wager, taking no further part in the hand. This assumes that no natural has been dealt. In blackjack, the introduction of the surrender rule has shown that all sides benefit. The casinos benefit from the ordinary overuse of such an option. The players benefit because they are allowed to make their own decisions, regardless of how incorrect those decisions may be. The one player in one hundred who is skilled enough to use the option only in the right circumstances also benefits, although this will not allow him to threaten the casinos' profits, since the right circumstances to use such an option in baccarat are quite rare.

To help you analyze any further rule changes, I have provided a chart listing the probabilities of obtaining various totals:

Player's Score

0	= 8.2%
1	= 7%
2	= 7%
3	= 7%
4	= 7%
5	= 7%
6	= 14.25%
7	= 14.25%
8	= 4.75%
9	= 4.75%
Natural 8	= 9.5%
Natural 9	= 9.5%

Banker's Score

0	= 7.5%
1	= 6.4%
2	= 6.4%
3	= 6.7%
4	= 9.3%
5	= 10.25%
6	= 12.75%
7	= 13.6%
8	= 4.2%
9	= 4.2%
Natural 8	= 9.5%
Natural 9	= 9.5

	Percent of Total Hands	Combinations	Percent of Total	Chance in One Hand
0		7,140	14.71	6.80
1		4,608	9.50	10.52
2		4,584	9.44	10.58
3		4,608	9.50	10.58
4		4,584	9.44	10.58
5		4,608	9.50	10.52
6		4,584	9.44	10.58
7		4,608	9.50	10.52
8		4,584	9.44	10.58
9		4,608	9.50	10.52
		4,856		

I believe, however, that the main problem with the modern form of baccarat is that it does not give the player the opportunity to exercise even rudimentary playing options, while the former versions of the game do. This is an important aspect to the success of any gambling game, because the player who feels in control of his destiny is much more content than one who does not. Also, by allowing the play of a hand to be broken up, the player receives successive and heightened boosts of adrenaline, the "buzz" that makes gambling so appealing. This protracted tension is the reason why many more gamblers prefer games such as Let It Ride or blackjack to baccarat.

That skilled variants of baccarat such as Yin Yang Yo and Super Pan Nine have achieved a great deal of success in the card rooms of California and beyond suggests that the main version of the game would benefit from the addition of an opportunity to exercise drawing-and-standing decisions.

By reintroducing some element of skill, I believe the casinos would combine the popular appeal of games that demand skill with the higher wagers of baccarat. As the chapters on the former variations of baccarat reveal, adding an element of skill to the game is unlikely to give professional gamblers the ability to threaten the house edge seriously. It is much more likely that unskilled players will give the casinos greater profits than they currently enjoy.

APPENDIX A

GLOSSARY OF TERMS

Banco The banker.

Banker In Punto Banco, whoever currently holds the shoe is designated the banker. The shoe is passed around the table counterclockwise to the right of the dealer every time the bank hand loses. This is of ceremonial importance only. In former versions of the game the banker had certain advantageous drawing-and-standing options and had to cover the wagers of the other players.

Banker Hand The banker's hand is a two- or three-card total, which pays off any wagers bet on its success at 19 to 20, or 0.95, should it be closer to a total of 9 than the player hand.

Bankroll The total amount of money you are willing to risk at the casino.

Cut-Card A plastic yellow card (not a playing card) is provided for the player who, at the dealer's invitation, inserts it into the stack of cards after they have been shuffled. Following this "cut," the cards are placed in the shoe ready for dealing. Its use counters any possibility of a dealer stacking the deck in favor of the players, allowing them to win money swiftly and splitting the profits with the colluding croupier.

False Draw An error by the banker or player in standing or drawing a third card. Not in compliance with the rules of play.

High Roller A term derived from games using dice, but used to describe any gambler who bets large sums. In baccarat, one suggested definition of a large sum was $10,000 on a hand; this was in the early 1990s. The term usually implies wealth and social position, along with other aspects of a glamorous or notorious lifestyle.

House Edge The percentage, on average, of money placed as bets which will be gained by the casino. For example, if the house edge on the banker bet in baccarat is 1.06 percent, and $1 million is wagered in many banker bets over a period, the casino would expect to collect a sum close to $10,600.

Natural   A total of 8 or 9.

Player   Whoever makes the largest wager on the player's side of the table.

Player Hand   The player's hand is a two- or three-card total which pays off any wagers bet on its success at 1 to 1, should it be closer to a total of 9 than the player's hand.

Punto   The "player."

Push   This occurs when hands tie, so bets on the player or banker hand are void.

Rules of Play   The rules determining whether the banker or the player draws a third card.

Scorecards   See "tally sheets."

Shill   An employee of the casino who sits at a gaming table posing as a gambler in order to encourage visitors to join in the game.

Shoe   The box into which the cards are placed after being shuffled and cut, and from which they are taken during the game.

Streak   Any series of repeated wins by either the banker or player.

Tally Sheets   Sheets of lined paper or a card provided so that players may record the fall of cards and their wins and losses.

Tie   When the value of the banker hand equals the player hand. All bets on the banker or player are considered a push when this happens.

Tie Bet   In Punto Banco and mini-baccarat, a bet that the deal will produce a tie between the player and banker hands. The house pays out at 8 to 1 if a tie results.

AN EVALUATION OF THE LITERATURE

The often unhelpful and misleading advice offered by many books concerning baccarat contributes to the relatively low standard of play at the tables. Books aimed at the mass market are usually of poor quality, and a player seeking genuine, useful information has to seek out works of a statistical or mathematical nature, find an out-of-print work, or browse through general works on gambling for specific information on baccarat, in order to gain any information of value.

The following titles, all published in the United States, are some you are bound to come across sooner or later. The majority are simple how-to guides or basic descriptions of the game, accompanied by a selection of baccarat lore, and sometimes include a few well-established gambling fallacies. Here are some of the most recent, and also some of the most interesting:

Barnhart, Russell. *Bankers Strategy at Baccara Chemin-de-Fer, Baccarat-en-Banque and Nevada Baccarat.* Las Vegas, 1980.

Unparalleled insight into the three incarnations of the game from one of the best gambling writers in the world. The only detailed study of the European variations of the game. Unfortunately, very hard to find.

Cardoza, Avery. *The Basics of Winning Baccarat.* Cardoza Publishing, New York, 1992.

An inexpensive description of the various forms of baccarat and the associated customs of baccarat. A good introduction to the game, lacking unnecessary material. Explains the basics of card-counting.

Professor Hoffman. *Baccarat Fair and Foul.* Casino Press, Atlantic City, NJ, 1983.

Detailed description of the frauds perpetrated by cheaters at the former forms of baccarat at the end of the last century. Originally published in 1891, this is a classic work of interest chiefly to students of the history of the game.

Patrick, John. *John Patrick's Baccarat: How to Play and Win at the Table With the Fastest Action and the Highest Stakes.* Lyle Stuart, Secaucus, NJ, 1997.

Patrick extolls the virtues of money management, discipline, the importance of an adequate bankroll, and reliable knowledge of the game, all of which is fair enough; but he encourages the use of "regression" betting methods. Much of the material is identical to other books in the Patrick gambling series.

Qui, John. *Q's Winning Baccarat Strategies.* Gambler's Book Club, New York, 1998.

Qui suggests a system to use when you are betting on the tie. He says, "some shoes are rich in ties...others are scarce." He backs up his point with diagrams and charts plus his own questionable logic. This book is certainly interesting, but it is terrible to think anyone might actually put Qui's methods into practice. Qui states that because the tie is often set at a lower minimum than the other wagers, a player who bets small has a better chance. Of course, the opposite is true: the greater than 14 percent edge will eat up an inadequately financed player in no time, Qui's ideas about locating a "tie-rich" shoe notwithstanding. Qui's understanding of baccarat falls significantly beneath complete ignorance of the game. A gambler who consistently bets on the tie loses fourteen times faster than a gambler who bets on the player or the bank—it's that simple.

Renzoni, Tommy. *Baccarat: Everything You Wanted to Know About Playing And Winning.* Lyle Stuart, Secaucus, NJ, 1997.

An entertaining, informative, and enthusiastic treatment of the game from the man who introduced the modern game to the United States. Interesting for its historical and human interest value.

St. Germain, Erick. *Seventy-two days at the Baccarat Table (Live! Mini-bac Decisions).* Zumma Publishing Co., Zumma, CA, 1995.

The award for stamina at mini-baccarat tables goes to this author, who collated data from forty-five thousand hands of mini-baccarat play, or a total of six hundred entire shoes. A streak analysis chart for each shoe is given. The author is to be admired for his tenacity, but his research would have been more helpful if it had been undertaken with those interested in scientific systems in mind, as well as the average player.

This book has been indirectly responsible for a resurgence in interest in betting progressions. Ian Harmer, who promotes a progression system known as "turnaround" on the Internet, cited the Zumma data as evidence that his method works. Harmer, and others like him, can draw such a conclusion because forty-five thousand hands, while requiring a great deal of time to record, is not a statistically significant sample. With such a sample, there is bound to be a system which wins consistently against *this* particular set of hands, but that system won't work for the next forty-five thousand hands you play. Such is the danger of placing too much faith in real-world statistics. Despite this, it's a good idea to browse through the data if only to get a feel of what happens in an average session of baccarat. The data also confirms that the real-world game is pretty much identical to the computer-generated one, and the figures given for the house advantage calculated by computer are borne out by this sample.

Stuart, Lyle. *Lyle Stuart on Baccarat.* Barricade Books, New York, 1998.

Stuart is one of the most influential writers on modern baccarat, and in many ways that's no bad thing. In this revised edition his anecdotes are entertaining, and his advice is often suitable. I cannot agree with his belief in trending (his "rule of three" has recently become one of the most popular systems). Then again, the 70-plus-year-old Stuart does not need my approval; he had recently won $245,000 in successive baccarat tournaments in Atlantic City, one at Bally's Grand Hotel and one at the Taj Mahal.

Tamburin, Henry and Rahm, Dick. *The First Effective Card-counting Systems for the Casino Game of Baccarat.* Research Services, Mobile, 1983.

Prior to the publication of this book, Rahm and Tamburin's work was far and away the best treatment of the mathematics of the game. Although it uses layman's terms, it nonetheless deals with the more sophisticated aspects of the game. Rahm and Tamburin believed that the game could not be beaten by card-counting, and their system is designed to minimize losses for the player. Contains an interesting chapter explaining the fallacious nature of betting systems. An essential purchase for the serious student of the game.

Wong, Stanford. *Casino Tournament Strategy.* Pi Yee Press, La Jolla, CA, 1997.

The only worthwhile study of correct strategy for gambling tournaments which is available. The book has sections on blackjack, keno, craps, and horse tourneys, but the section on baccarat makes it worth purchasing even if you only play this game. This book will allow you to win double the amount you pay, on average, in entry fees.

General Gambling Texts

Surprisingly, the best information to be found about baccarat is not in books about the game. Some of those mentioned below may devote less than a dozen pages to the subject, but they often impart much more useful information than works specifically devoted to the subject:

Epstein, Richard. *The Theory of Gambling and Statistical Logic.* Academic Press, San Diego, CA, 1995.

While you would have to be a degree-level mathematician to fully understand this book, it is nonetheless worthwhile for any level of gambler to read. This recently reprinted classic from the 1960s touches on baccarat only briefly, and Epstein deals only with the chemin de fer form of baccarat. Nevertheless, he gives a clear explanation of how the drawing-and-standing rules were arrived at, as well as a fascinating glimpse of the origins of the game, and it contains extremely useful information on various methods of gambling, including a method to predict cards following a shuffle, that may be of great value if applied to baccarat. Some of Epstein's suggestions have tortured and inspired professional gamblers for years. This is pretty much the unvarnished truth about games of chance. Try to borrow it from a library.

Rubin, Max. *Comp City.* Huntingdon Press, Las Vegas, 1994.

Essential reading for the big table baccarat player, who automatically falls into the class of gambler who can benefit most from casino comps. Rubin was an insider who's played both sides of the tables and knows how to beat the system. After reading the book, the well-financed player should be able to get free rooms, travel, and tickets to the best Las Vegas shows, and, ultimately, a free vacation.

Scott, Jean. *The Frugal Gambler.* Huntingdon Press, Las Vegas, 1998.

This book is to the low-rolling afficianado what *Comp City* is to the big-table player. Scott describes how she takes a vacation in Nevada for months on end with the casinos paying her way. In a well-written and entertaining style, Scott describes how she prizes the value from slot coupon books and comps. The chapter where she explains how to get free flights is alone worth the cost of the book, which pays for itself many times over. Note that Scott plays mostly 25-cent video poker; there is nothing directly aimed at the baccarat player. But most of the techniques described here are universal to all casino games, and would be of special interest to mini-baccarat players.

Thorp, Edward. *The Mathematics of Gambling.* Lyle Stuart, Secaucus, NJ, 1985.

Contains a description of the first primitive attempts to analyze the modern game of baccarat back in the 1960s. Describes in detail, and in layman's terms, how Thorp attempted to see if a linear card-counting system could beat the game. Also valuable for Thorp's explanation and proof that all betting progression systems devised do not change the odds, including those that have not yet been created, of which there are an infinite number.

Wilson, Alan. *The Casino Gambler's Guide.* HarperCollins, New York, 1970.

This book was ahead of its time and still outranks the vast majority of gambling literature. Wilson was possessed of a visionary mind which allowed him to anticipate the advent of successful gambling systems. Provides a detailed chapter on baccarat which clearly explains why a card-counting system cannot overcome the house edge, and describes the Thorp-Walden team's attempt to beat the "natural" side bets. Priceless.

Appendix C

The Floating Edge

The explanation for this phenomenon is complex, and not by any means complete. At very extreme negative counts, say, for example, when all the cards in the deck are 10s (as in the previous example suggested by Roger Gros), our count system tells us we are playing with a disadvantage. According to Griffin, the removal of a 10 decreases the house advantage on the tie bet, so a deck composed only of 10s would have a very low count. If only 10s remain, however, as Gros previously pointed out, we are playing with an 800 percent advantage! At the other extreme, high counts also gives us a huge advantage. A deck composed only of 5s (whose effect of removal is bad) also gives us an advantage of 800 percent. These extreme situations become more commonplace as we get deeper into the deck. For this to result in no change in our overall expectation for the whole shoe, there must be some kind of balancing force around our count system's pivot at 0. Could we then use a higher figure to determine at which point we have the advantage? Yes, and it gives us a slight advantage over the house, but our average earnings per hour are still at minimum-wage levels with anything other than obscene, you-could-buy-a-hospital-with-that-sort-of-money wagers.

It's also possible that extremely negative counts, as well as extremely positive ones, might be worth wagering on. It seems intuitively likely that there is some point at which the composition of remaining cards becomes so concentrated in negative cards that the number of possible totals becomes limited, thereby creating increased expectation for the tie bettor.

Appendix D

How to Bet When the Player Has the Advantage

Given that the highly skilled player can occasionally detect situations in which the odds are in his favor, how should he bet?

He could bet his entire bankroll. Say a player did this, and the total of his bankroll is $5,000. Every time he gets a 20 percent advantage by, for example, determining a deck composition which gives the tie approximately this advantage, he can expect to make $1,000 overall. In effect, he "earns" this amount, a very attractive return. But hang on a minute! The tie bet only occurs, on average, less than once in every ten deals! The tie bet, of necessity, must occur more frequently if the card-counter detects an advantage, but even in the most favorable situations it will usually occur less than one time in five. In this example, the tie will *not* occur 87 percent of the time. So the gambler has an 87 percent chance of losing everything. He might well have an advantage in the long run, but that's academic—he won't be able to continue playing with no money.

Alternatively, the player could pursue the other extreme and bet the table minimum. This virtually guarantees that he will not be ruined before he gets ahead *when he has the advantage*, but the money he wins from the occasional favorable situation will not outweigh the considerable losses from the unfavorable bets he must place in order to stay in the game. Consequently, he is playing a losing game. Even if he watches from the sidelines and only bets when the deck is positive, he will win so slowly that working at McDonald's would seem attractive by comparison.

So, the gambler is caught between the devil and the deep blue sea. Fortunately, an effective compromise exists. This was suggested by John L. Kelly many years ago in an article in the *Bell System Technical Journal*. Kelly presented a problem: say a telegraph operator learns the result of a horse race and delays the information long enough to go down to his local bookmakers and place a wager before betting is closed. How much of his money should he bet? Kelly says all of it. From this simple example he derives what has become known as the Kelly Criterion. This means that the best betting strategy, i.e., the best balance between fast gains and low risk of ruin, is to bet the percentage of your bankroll in proportion to the advantage you enjoy. So a gambler with $1,000 who finds a bet with a 1 percent advantage should ideally wager $10.

Theoretically, you could never go bust with the Kelly Criterion, since you are always wagering a fixed fraction of your capital, never the total amount, unless you are betting with 100 percent certainty. In the real world, of course, casinos and bookmakers will not let you divide your bet infinitely and will only accept certain convenient minimum amounts, and therefore you must apply some dialectic logic. Thus, it is impossible to use perfect Kelly betting, although using the best approximation of the Kelly Criterion is almost as effective.

It is always to your financial disadvantage to deviate from Kelly. The bettor who wagers twice the Kelly Criterion is doomed to see his bankroll spiral endlessly up and down, going nowhere. Even though he is playing with an advantage, he will never fully exploit it.

So, how do we apply Kelly to baccarat? Well, it depends on what we are betting on. First we must know how to use Kelly with uneven payoffs. We must divide the Kelly bet by the ratio of a winning wager (with the tie 8) by a losing wager (1). So if we detect a 72 percent advantage for the draw and have a bankroll of $1,000, we divide 72 by 8, giving 9 percent as the correct fraction of our bankroll to bet, or $90.

Such a betting scheme would be perfect if we only bet when we had the advantage. We may, however, have to make some bad wagers, which is usually the case if we are card-counting or using a method to analyze the shuffle, since our techniques don't give us an edge on every hand.

This, in effect, is a "tax" which drains away the expected value of the infrequent favorable bets. With an unfavorable wager, the Kelly system recommends a negative bet, or a bet on the house, which we can't do (much as we'd like to). The best compromise is to bet the table minimum.

Gambling theorists have recently recognized that in a series of positive and negative expectation wagers, the combined expectation of both types of wager must be considered. Therefore, we must bet more conservatively than a straight application of Kelly would suggest. In *The Mathematics of Gambling*, Thorp suggests that to counter the attrition of the series of negative expectation wagers, a player should bet only three-quarters of a pure Kelly system. This suggestion was made with regard to blackjack, where the frequency of favorable situations is much higher than in baccarat. When the baccarat deck is favorable, however, it is much more favorable than a blackjack deck would be. Moreover, bets in blackjack can become very unfavorable indeed, whereas bets in baccarat remain fairly static around the 1 percent house edge, as we have seen. Therefore, I suggest that Thorp's proposition is equally valid for baccarat. This is a pretty crude approximation, and the precise amount to bet depends on how many bad wagers we make relative to the good ones, and this will depend greatly on the technique we are using and the form of baccarat we are playing.

It is clear that the player should not use any betting scheme that does not give him a positive expectation, i.e., that does not allow him to win more than he loses. It is therefore essential to find a balance between profitability and an acceptably small risk of loss.